Amazing But

Amazing
But True

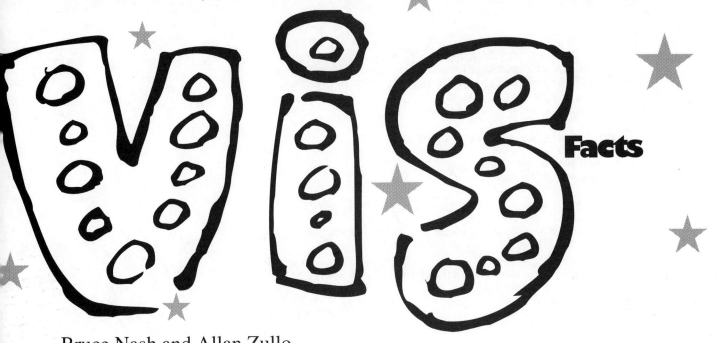

Vis Facts

Bruce Nash and Allan Zullo

With John McGran

ANDREWS AND MCMEEL • *A Universal Press Syndicate Company* • KANSAS CITY

For information, write Andrews and McMeel,
a Universal Press Syndicate Company,
4900 Main Street, Kansas City, Missouri 64112.

Designed by Rick Cusick
Illustrations by Paul Coker

Library of Congress Cataloging-in-Publication Data

Nash, Bruce M.
    Amazing but true Elvis facts / Bruce Nash and Allan Zullo : with John McGran.
      p.   cm.
    ISBN: 0–8362–7028–2
    1. Presley, Elvis, 1935–1977—Miscellanea.   I. Zullo, Allan.
  II. McGran, John.   III. Title.
  ML420.P96N37   1995   94–45515
  782.42166'092—dc20   CIP
  [B]   MN

To Pat Lee and John Moffitt, two extraordinary people who best personify the meaning of the word "class." Your experience has taught me, your dedication has inspired me, and your friendship has enriched me.

— Bruce Nash

To Sasha Nicole. It's now or never. Follow that dream.

—Allan Zullo

Contents

Hail to the King

although Elvis Presley took his last breath on August 16, 1977, he continues to live—in his music, in his movies, and in our memories.

He was the undisputed King of Rock 'n' Roll. No performer in the twentieth century has left such an astounding legacy of fame—more than one billion records sold, televised concerts and thirty-one films seen by over a billion fans around the globe, and more than four billion dollars' worth of Elvis Presley merchandise sold. More books have been written about the King than any other entertainer in the world.

And yet there is much that fans don't know about the greatest rock 'n' roller of all time.

For instance, did you know that Elvis:

* was called "old Super Ears" by his classmates because he could listen to other people's conversations while he was talking?

* held pajama parties with three thirteen-year-old girls at Graceland when he was nineteen years old?

* performed a concert while packing two pistols—one in his boot and another in his waistband?

* once ate five ice cream sundaes for breakfast and passed out?

* hatched a plot to personally murder several drug dealers in Memphis?

* believed that the ghost of his mother roamed the hallways of Graceland?

* once took off over $200,000 worth of his own jewelry and gave it away to a dozen stunned fans at a concert?

* was offered the title role in the Oscar-winning film *Midnight Cowboy*?

* had a premonition of his death just days before he died?

This book reveals hundreds of incredible but true Elvis facts from his birth to his death—and even beyond the grave.

There has never been a performer like Elvis Presley. There will never be one like him ever again. He truly was amazing.

Before He Was King

School Daze

Almost without fail, Elvis would be accompanied on his daily walk to school by his overprotective mother, Gladys, during his grade school days in Tupelo, Mississippi.

The ritual became somewhat of an embarrassment to Elvis when it continued into his high school years after the family moved to Memphis.

* * *

Presley's classmates in Tupelo called him "old Super Ears" because he had hearing so sharp that he could listen to other people's conversations while he was talking.

* * *

Like most kids, Elvis enjoyed reading comic books, especially about superheroes such as Batman and Superman. In fact, they inspired Elvis later in life. "I was the hero of every comic book I ever read," admitted Elvis.

1

Captain Marvel and Captain Marvel Jr. were his favorites, so it wasn't surprising when Elvis later tailored his look to match their image. The sweeping capes, glistening hairstyles, and assertive stance were a direct result of his "marvel-ous" role models.

* * *

For his eleventh birthday, Elvis asked for a shotgun. He didn't get it. Instead, his mother bought him a guitar. Although he was disappointed at first, Presley quickly changed his tune. He began to practice the chords that he learned from his Uncle Vester, First Assembly minister Reverend Smith, and local country star Mississippi Slim, host of a live show on WELO radio.

* * *

Financial problems forced the Presleys to leave Tupelo for Memphis, one hundred miles away. On his last day of school in Tupelo, Elvis brought his guitar to class and gave a farewell performance. He sang "Leaf on a Tree."

The family moved into an apartment owned by a rabbi who lived upstairs. Elvis spent eighth grade at the Christine School and then enrolled at L.C. Humes High School.

His music teacher, Elsie Marmann, told Elvis he wasn't a very good singer because he sang off key. She claimed that Presley "didn't have the kind of voice I could use in a glee club."

* * *

In high school, Elvis stood apart from the others by his appearance. He wore colorful western outfits and outlandish colors like pink and kelly green. As a result, he was ridiculed by the other kids who considered him a dumb hillbilly. It didn't help matters that he also suffered from a bad case of acne.

When he was sixteen, he started growing his hair long, high in front and sweeping at the sides into a D.A. at the back. He was so particular about his hair that he didn't go to a regular barber. Instead, he got his long hair trimmed by a local female beautician.

* * *

A classmate, James Ausborn, once told a reporter that Elvis often took him to the cemetery to visit Presley's twin brother, Jesse, who died in childbirth. "He would go burdened and low," Ausborn recalled. "Elvis would look at the grave and talk a little to Jesse—and after the visit, he was always jolly and lifted in spirits."

* * *

Elvis was an end on the Humes High Tigers football team in his sophomore year in high school. However, his mother made him quit the squad because she was worried he would get hurt.

* * *

During his senior year at Humes High, Elvis was encouraged by his teacher Mildred Scrivener to perform at the school's annual minstrel show. He sang "Keep Them Cold Icy Fingers Off of Me." Elvis garnered more applause than any other performer and was brought back for an encore, for which he sang "Till I Waltz Again with You." (On the program for the April 9, 1953, show, the guitar-playing performer was listed as Elvis "Prestly.")

"They really like me, Miss Scrivener, they really like me!" an excited Elvis shouted to his teacher afterward.

* * *

Although kids in school liked his singing, they didn't want to become Presley's friends. But there was one girl who enjoyed being with him—his first real sweetheart, Dixie Locke. "She was kind of small with long dark hair that came down to her shoulders and the biggest smile I've ever seen anywhere," Presley once recalled. "She was always laughing, always enjoying herself. I gave her my high school ring. For two years we had a ball."

Presley's parents assumed the two would eventually get married. But when Elvis launched his singing career, he was gone from home for long periods of time. While he was away, Dixie fell in love with someone else. She didn't have the heart to tell Elvis it was over, so she asked his mother Gladys to break the news to him. The breakup crushed Elvis.

A Star Is Born

On July 5, 1954, Elvis recorded his first songs for record producer Sam Phillips—"That's All Right (Mama)" and "Blue Moon of Kentucky." Two days later, on disc jockey Dewey Phillips's show "Red, White, and Blue," Elvis's "That's All Right (Mama)" was played fourteen times. The station received forty-seven phone calls from listeners who loved the record.

Dewey Phillips then tried to reach Elvis for an interview. But Presley, who was too embarrassed to listen to the song on the radio, was in the movie theater watching *The Best*

Years of Our Lives. His father, Vernon, rushed to the theater and got Elvis, who hustled over to the radio station for his interview.

Several weeks later, a *Billboard* review labeled Elvis as a "strong new talent." Elvis gave notice at Crown Electric, where he worked as a truck driver, and within days performed in his first real concert at the Overton Park Band Shell in Memphis.

He was so good that he became an unannounced performer at another show there featuring several top country and western singers. Recalled Presley, "When I went on, I made myself forget about me and gave it all I had. Suddenly, the teenagers in the back of the audience started screaming. I finished, and they screamed louder and louder. I was scared. I didn't understand it. But when I knew they were screaming *for* me, I felt something big and wonderful had begun."

Presley's hip-shaking versions of "Good Rockin' Tonight" and "That's All Right (Mama)" wowed the audience so much that veteran singer Webb Pierce was miffed. He refused to follow such a dynamite performance because he knew he couldn't possibly top it.

By the end of the year, Elvis was voted "No. 1 Most Promising New Star" at the annual C&W Disc Jockeys Convention.

In the fall of 1955, Sun Records sold the rights to Presley—a future star who eventually would sell over one billion records—to RCA Victor for the paltry sum of only $40,000. Elvis received a $5,000 bonus in the deal.

Among the first things Presley bought with the money were new clothes and a pink Cadillac for his parents, and two Mixmasters for his mother. "I want my mama to have two of them so we can put them on each end of the kitchen counter and it'll cut down on all the walking she has to do," he told the clerk.

On January 27, 1956, Presley's "Heartbreak Hotel" was released. By April, it won him his first "Triple Crown" award from *Billboard*, having hit No. 1 on the pop, rhythm and blues, and country and western charts. It was only the second time in record history that such a feat had been accomplished. (The first was Carl Perkins's hit "Blue Suede Shoes," which Elvis later recorded.)

"[Singing] is a way of caressing people with your voice."

Don't Quit Your Day Job

Singin' the Blues

Contrary to popular belief, Elvis was not an instant sensation. In fact, his singing turned off a lot of people when he first started out.

Official transcripts from Humes High School in Memphis show that even Elvis's music teacher didn't think much of his unique singing style. The eager entertainer who would go on to enthrall tens of millions of devoted fans took home a report card with a so-so "C" in his music studies.

Elvis was still trying to make the grade in 1953 when, at the age of seventeen, he turned to the church and Rev. James E. Hamill, who was organizing a gospel quartet. Presley performed with as much passion as he could muster and belted out what he believed to be a terrific performance at the First Assembly of God church.

But the energized teen didn't have a prayer. Hamill wasn't the least bit impressed by the skinny white boy's soulful servings of gospel music. The Presley family's pastor took it upon himself to call Elvis aside and urge the boy to "give it up" when it came to singing for the Lord.

Ironically, gospel music would later produce some of Presley's most memorable and stirring songs. He never held a grudge against Hamill's rejection. In fact, five years later, Elvis asked the very same minister to conduct the funeral services for his mother, Gladys.

In 1954, when Elvis launched his music career, he was turned down by several club owners in the South who didn't think the young unknown was worth the hundred and fifty dollars a night he and his band were asking.

On September 25, 1954, Elvis made his first—and only—appearance onstage at the legendary Grand Ole Opry. The Nashville site was—and still is—nirvana for country warblers, so an ecstatic Elvis figured his show biz ship had finally come in.

But his performance at the hallowed hall was too quirky for the die-hard country music audience. The flashy clothes and greasy hair were hardly the style of the conservative Opry crowd.

Emcee and talent coordinator Jim Denny met Elvis backstage and offered him some stinging advice: "Go back to your former job as a truck driver." Presley was crushed by the negative response and he cried all the way home to Memphis. Despite Denny's ego-shattering assessment, Elvis stuck to his dream.

Elvis proved to be Mr. Persistence. He got a few breaks and was beginning to makes waves throughout the South when he boarded his first plane flight in March 1955.

The singer and fellow band members Scotty Moore and Bill Black headed to New York City, where they auditioned for a prized spot on the highly popular TV show "Arthur Godfrey's Talent Scouts."

Unfortunately, Elvis's dynamic set of songs didn't impress the show's talent coordinator. Presley's high-energy act was passed over for another up-and-coming talent—Pat Boone. The trip back to Memphis was an extremely somber one for the disappointed young men.

Elvis overcame his "Talent Scouts" rejection and returned to New York on January 28, 1956, for his first nationally televised appearance on Jimmy and Tommy Dorsey's variety series, "Stage Show." But it still wasn't an appreciation of his talent that landed Elvis his shot on TV. It was his good looks. The moment the impressed producer laid eyes on Elvis, the man gushed, "He's a guitar-playing Marlon Brando!"

In the spring of 1956, Americans were finally beginning to take a closer look at the brash young rocker with the funny first name. Agents and managers saw plenty of financial potential as they battled for bookings.

Suddenly, someone thought the showy singer would be a natural for the glamour and glitz of Las Vegas. Hotel manager Sammy Lewis hired Elvis to work for $12,500 a week for four weeks. However, Presley's first visit to the oasis in the desert would quickly prove to be a major bomb for the entertainer billed as "The Atomic-Powered Singer."

As one of the opening acts for the Freddie Martin Orchestra, Elvis discovered his patented moves failed to excite the stuffy Vegas audiences. The New Frontier Hotel lounge was so deathly quiet that the amazed musicians could actually hear themselves play— unlike when they performed before screaming, arm-flailing fans.

It was such an unsettling experience at this heartbreak hotel that after two weeks of snoozy shows, Elvis and the casino bigwigs agreed to end the gig, slicing his four-week engagement in half. Presley's spot on the musical menu was filled by songstress Roberta Sherwood and statuesque torch singer Jana Mason.

Presley's agent, Col. Tom Parker, got his embattled boy back in the national spotlight on July 1, 1956, as a special guest on Steve Allen's Sunday night TV variety show. The booking seemed like a good one for both the show and the rising young star. But Allen apparently had other plans.

The funnyman didn't approve of the public's overwhelming adulation of Elvis and he set out to embarrass the singer on national television. Most critics agree that Allen was doing his smug best to diminish his guest.

Elvis began on a good note by cranking out a dandy version of his new hit single, "I Want You, I Need You, I Love You." But then, at Allen's

insistence, Elvis, who was tastefully attired in a snazzy tux and blue suede shoes, performed his smash song "Hound Dog" to a basset hound that was wearing a top hat and bow tie and perched on a stool. An embarrassed Elvis somehow managed to offer an intense and witty version of the tune while singing to the silly-looking dog.

Fans were doggone mad that their singing idol was forced to serenade a real-life hound dog on "The Steve Allen Show." Although the studio audience had howled with laughter, millions of Elvis fans were outraged by a stunt they considered to be beneath their beloved King. Complaints from irate fans flooded the show and pickets sprang up outside the network offices the very next day. But Elvis, always the gentleman, took it all in stride and never accused Allen of any wrongdoing.

The protests proved one thing: Elvis mania had arrived.

Stepping on His Blue Suede Shoes

Even during his fantastic rise to fame, Elvis was criticized by so-called experts who failed to appreciate his unique singing style.

One of those extremely unimpressed with the singer was television impresario Ed Sullivan. The stone-faced host could easily make or break a new act. Appearing on Sullivan's variety show provided valuable exposure before millions of viewers.

Sullivan wanted no part of Elvis. In fact, he once vowed that he'd keep the rebellious rocker off his stage. But CBS network chiefs saw things differently. They went ahead and booked the crowd-pleasing singer for his first appearance on the Sullivan show on September 9, 1956.

The humbled host failed to appear for that ground-breaking show. Filling in for "ill" Ed was master of ceremonies Charles Laughton. Elvis took a step closer toward superstardom when the ratings went through the roof. An estimated 82.6 percent of the entire television viewing audience was tuned in to watch the singer strut his stuff. The astonishing rating meant that a whopping 54 million people were glued to their sets for the first Elvis appearance on "The Ed(less) Sullivan Show."

CBS so loved Presley's performance that the network bigwigs quickly booked Elvis for a return engagement on October 28. This time a somber Sullivan was there to present the King to his TV audience. Once again most Americans were mesmerized by Elvis.

On January 6, 1957, the now wildly popular singer returned for a smash third appearance on "The Ed Sullivan Show." America's love for the singing sensation was officially in full bloom.

But this time the giant home-viewing audience would get a different look at

the performer. Cautious CBS censors ordered all cameramen to film Elvis only from above the waist, so viewers couldn't see his gyrating hips as they had during his first two appearances on the show. The network knuckled under to increasing pressure from religious organizations and other uptight people who were shocked by Presley's patented pelvic thrusts. Elvis learned of the close-up conspiracy before he went onstage and still managed to steal the show by belting out seven smash songs—a record for the Sullivan show—including "Hound Dog" and "Don't Be Cruel."

The teen idol took home $50,000 for his three appearances, and CBS enjoyed its biggest ratings bonanza ever.

* * *

Another celebrity forced to swallow his pride and take part in the nation's celebration of Elvis was feisty Frank Sinatra. In 1957, Ol' Blue Eyes had termed rock 'n' roll "Phony and false—and written and played for the most part by cretinous goons."

Three years later, Frank shelled out $125,000 for Elvis to appear on his show for less than ten minutes. It was the first TV show Presley appeared on after his discharge from the army.

How Low Can He Go

During much of the 1960s, Elvis stopped singing in public and instead turned his attention to feature films. By the end of the decade the music world had pretty much passed him by, and it looked like the end was near for Presley's career.

However, Elvis made a dramatic comeback in 1968—but only after he was forced to witness an ego-devastating, humiliating experience.

With Presley's singing career in the doldrums, Col. Parker arranged for Elvis to do a TV Christmas special on NBC. The original idea was for Presley to sing standard Christmas carols and offer a typical Merry Christmas wish at the end. Fortunately, producer Steve Binder had a better idea. He wanted the Elvis of old, the rebel who had changed the face of rock 'n' roll music years earlier.

Presley and Parker weren't convinced that approach was necessary. After all, Elvis was the King.

Binder had to show Elvis he'd become a forgotten star to his fans. So the bold producer took a big chance and dared Elvis to stand on a busy Los Angeles street in broad daylight just so he could gauge the public reaction. Presley was hesitant, but he finally joined Binder in front of a club on the famous Sunset Strip. The result was a big blow to Elvis's ego. For fifteen minutes, the stunned singer stood in front of a topless bar and began talking loudly to attract attention to himself. No one noticed.

"Four o'clock in the afternoon and there we were, standing outside a topless bar," recalled Binder. "We stood there to the point of embarrassment. Kids were bumping into us and saying 'excuse me' or not even saying that. Elvis started talking louder than normal, trying to be recognized or noticed or something. But nothing happened. Nothing. Zero."

Elvis was convinced. He said, "Bah! Humbug!" to the Christmas theme and took the show in an exciting new direction. From that moment on, it was forget Christmas; the theme of this spectacular would be the rebirth of the King of Rock 'n' Roll. Binder had Presley dress in a black leather jacket and perform in a theater in the round with the audience—mostly women—sitting up close. Elvis looked and performed like the star of old.

The dynamite extravaganza became a sizzling showcase for Elvis and thrust a recharged Presley back in the limelight. The King had regained his throne.

The Evil Elvis

The FBI kept a thick, 663-page file on Elvis for more than twenty years. The bureau started the file because of fears that Presley would corrupt the youth of America.

FBI agents closely watched Elvis from practically the moment he first appeared on "The Ed Sullivan Show" in 1956 until his sudden death in 1977. Agents reported on everything

17

from the way Elvis dressed and gyrated on stage, to his private life and loves, to the many people who tried to cash in on his phenomenal fame.

Although many fans considered Elvis a heavenly dream come true, many others— including the feds—considered him a demon out to undermine the nation and warp its young women.

A 1956 memo to the FBI from a former member of army intelligence warned that the singer was "a definite danger to the security of the United States" because of his influence on youth.

Referring to a concert by Presley in Wisconsin, the memo stated, "One eyewitness described his [Elvis's] actions as 'a striptease with clothes on.' "

Elvis once faced the threat of arrest if he swiveled his hips during a performance.

In Jacksonville, Florida, in 1955, police were ordered to film an Elvis performance to see if the pelvis-pivoting singer was committing some sort of lewd public offense. Judge Marion Gooding went so far as to prepare arrest warrants in advance. The on-duty officers had strict orders to pull the plug on Presley's show and cart him off to jail if he dared move his body in a way deemed threatening to the morals of those in the audience.

Alerted in advance, Elvis coolly avoided jail by toning down his act just enough to pass muster with the prudish police and Judge Gooding during both sellout concerts.

Even with a slightly less frenzied performance, Presley discovered there were few safe havens from his overzealous fans. An untamed mob stormed Elvis's dressing room following his first Jacksonville concert. The crazed crowd burst into his room and literally stripped the surprised singer of his clothes. Overwhelmed security needed reinforcements to bring the swarm of screaming fans under control.

Elvis managed to remain calm throughout the backstage mugging. He came away more amused than frightened and even insisted his fans didn't mean him any harm. Presley figured his awestruck attackers were merely in search of personal mementos following a sensational show.

Such wild demonstrations didn't help the singer win fans in high places. In fact, during the height of Elvis hysteria in 1956, the state of New Jersey banned rock concerts to keep performers like him from corrupting the budding youth of the Garden State. That same year, a *New York Daily News* editorial urged a ban on public dancing. The paper suggested teens get written consent from their parents before dancing in the streets to a Presley tune.

Elvis also enraged the passionate folks of the religious right. In 1956, the head of a religious newspaper in Wisconsin issued a warning through a scathing letter to the editor: "Presley is a definite danger to the security of the United States. Eyewitnesses have told me that Presley's actions and motions were such as to rouse the sexual passions of teenaged youth. Presley signed autographs on a girl's abdomen. He has fan clubs that degenerate into sex orgies. I would judge that he may be both a drug addict and a sexual pervert."

Rev. Charles Howard Graff of St. John's Episcopal Church in Greenwich Village,

New York, used his pulpit to rail against Elvis in 1956. The righteous Graff warned his parish about the singing demon he labeled a "whirling dervish of sex."

Some churches managed to convince young members of their congregation to attend Presley's first movie, *Love Me Tender*, and interrupt the shows by heckling. In several cities, policemen were stationed inside the theaters to prevent further disorder.

O (No) Canada

In 1957, the anti-Elvis craziness spread to Canada, where eight girls were expelled from the Notre Dame Convent in Ottawa because they broke an oath to stay away from a Presley performance.

All of the students at the religious institution had signed a declaration that they would never attend one of the entertainer's sinful concerts. But eight of the girls couldn't resist such temptation and saw his show. They were kicked out of school when uptight officials discovered their dastardly deed.

Elvis made just two other appearances in Canada that year, both sellouts in Toronto and Vancouver. The popular singer was scheduled to take his tour to Montreal, but the Catholic church stepped in to douse the fires of sin and kept the city and its impressionable youth Presley-free.

The Red Menace

As if it wasn't bad enough getting attacked in his own country, Elvis was denounced by the Communists.

The East German Communist magazine *Youth World* claimed Elvis was a capitalistic tool and declared: "Elvis Presley is a weapon of the American psychological war aimed at inflicting a part of the population with a new philosophical outlook of inhumanity . . . to destroy anything that is beautiful in order to prepare for war."

Elvis got himself in hot water with Mexican Communists in 1957. An undercover FBI agent noted that the Communists were spreading a vicious, totally fabricated rumor that Elvis had said he "would rather kiss three black girls than one Mexican girl."

In an FBI memo, the G-man added: "It was said that [Elvis's] new dance rhythm would find no popular reception among the Mexican youth due to their strict upbringing and serious views. Then rock and roll began to catch on."

Fearing an Americanization of their country's youth, party members hastily organized a campaign to prevent Presley songs from being played on Mexico City radio. Morally minded university students were urged to put together protests in front of stores where Elvis magazines and recordings were sold. The protesters even held public burnings of the King's albums.

In late 1962, Mexico's Office of Public Entertainment announced it was banning Presley's movie *Blue Hawaii* from being shown south of the border. The harsh decree had nothing to do with the content of the movie. Officials were still stinging from the theater riot that broke out among fans during the screening of Elvis's previous movie, *G.I. Blues*. The manic moviegoers left the Americas Theater in Mexico City in shambles by tearing up seats and breaking windows.

All Shook Up

It wasn't only religious zealots or frightened politicians who cast disparaging words at Elvis. Respected personalities lambasted Presley too.

Some of his detractors and their critical comments included:

* Bing Crosby: "He hasn't contributed a damn thing to music."

* Steve Allen: "The fact that someone with so little ability became the most popular singer in history says something significant about our cultural standards."

* Jackie Gleason: "He can't last. I tell you flatly, he can't last." (Gleason made an about-face when he gave Presley his first shot on national TV on "Stage Show," which Gleason coproduced.)

* Rev. Billy Graham: "I wouldn't let my daughter walk across the street to see Elvis Presley perform."

* *New York Times* critic Jack Gould: "Mr. Presley has no discernible singing ability."

* *New York Herald Tribune* critic John Crosby: "Where do you go from Elvis Presley —short of obscenity, which is against the law."

* *San Francisco Chronicle* critic John L. Wasserman: "Extraordinarily untalented."

* * *

Famous gossip columnist Hedda Hopper also did her best to squelch Elvis mania. Hopper considered Presley a danger to society—or at least to young girls—and used her poison pen to get the point across. She spewed so much venom that readers may well have imagined they were reading about Satan himself.

One particularly nasty column noted: "I don't like Elvis Presley because I consider him a menace to young girls!" Another day, another holler: "He is the most obscene, vulgar influence on young America today."

Hopper's campaign of criticism failed miserably, and the adoring public helped bring the columnist back to reality. Realizing her readers didn't agree with her constant carping about the King, Hopper eventually became an Elvis fan. The cantankerous columnist soon couldn't squeeze enough good things about the singer into her gossipy ramblings.

"When you start out, they say you won't last.
And when you do, they try and get you to quit.
They get you coming and going."

The Show Must Go On

Vegas Death Threat

Elvis performed a Las Vegas concert while armed with a pair of guns—because he was the target of a death threat serious enough to bring in the FBI.

In 1970, an anonymous caller to the Las Vegas Hilton, where Presley was performing, said he wanted $50,000 to reveal the name of a "madman who was going to shoot Elvis with a silencer." Earlier, the same caller had warned that Elvis would be kidnapped, and offered to sell details of the plot.

A Hilton executive wanted to cancel the evening's two shows, but Elvis declined. "If some nut is determined to kill me, he won't stop tonight because I'm not there," Presley said. "No, I have to face it. I'm going on."

And Elvis made it clear that no one was to pay a dime to any extortionist. "If we pay one guy, we open the door for every nut in the world. It'll make it worse for people like Frank Sinatra, Neil Diamond, Wayne Newton, and other people who do shows. I won't have anything to do with it."

Authorities were called in to investigate. According to an FBI report of the matter, local police were providing protection to Presley's family, especially his wife, Priscilla, and their daughter, Lisa Marie. In addition to his regular armed guards, Elvis had doubled the force of hotel security.

After sticking a two-shot derringer pistol into his right boot and slipping a .45 into his waistband, Presley noted, "The hotel told me that I don't have to do the show. But I'm going to. I'd rather die onstage than in bed."

He then told his loyal bodyguards that if he were shot, they were to rip the assassin's eyes out. Bodyguard Jerry Schilling recalled that they came up with a plan of action in case of an attack. If Elvis heard a gunshot, he'd drop to the floor and some of his henchmen would cover him like a human shield. Others would then rush the gunman.

Schilling later told reporters that Elvis got a scare during the tense show when, "right in the middle, from up in the balcony, a guy hollers, 'Elvis!' Now this was very unusual. Usually it's the girls who holler."

The singer dropped to one knee and peered into the darkness of the crowd. Elvis then muttered "Yeah?" while waiting for the worst. But the man turned out to be a fan rather than a fanatic and he merely had a request for the King to sing "Don't Be Cruel."

Elvis was so relieved that he proceeded to belt out the tune even though he rarely took requests during his act. The would-be assassin never appeared, and the show ended like any other night.

* * *

The FBI also investigated a number of earlier death threats and extortion attempts aimed at the superstar.

In 1956, a scribbled postcard sent to Presley said, "If you don't stop this shit, we're going to kill you."

In 1959, the Pentagon alerted the FBI about a letter from a soldier in East Germany, who said the Red Army was hatching a plot to assassinate Presley.

In 1964, a scribbled letter sent to Elvis warned, "You will be next on my list."

The singer went onstage in Las Vegas in 1971 after finding a note in his hotel mail slot warning him to pay $50,000 or be shot.

The threatening letter was scrawled on a hotel ad that had a photo of Elvis on its front. Drawn on the picture was a pistol pointing at his heart. On the bottom was the message, "Guess who, and where?"

The FBI considered it a serious death threat, but it couldn't keep Elvis from entertaining that evening as scheduled.

When Elvis Was Conned

Elvis was once conned out of hundreds of thousands of dollars by crafty gangsters.

According to the FBI file on Presley, an elaborate con job cost Elvis his Jetstar plane and perhaps $400,000. The official file stated that several mob-connected crooks "bought" the luxury aircraft with checks that bounced. They then mortgaged the plane for one million dollars and got Elvis to pay another $400,000 for repairs that were never made.

The gang, which was known as the Fraternity by its members, was described by the FBI as "thirty to forty of the world's top con men." The high-flying scheme was eventually squashed, and several members were convicted. But Elvis died before the Jetstar and most of his money were returned to Graceland.

The Extortion Scheme That Failed

A doctor once tried to blackmail Elvis.

In 1959, South African dermatologist Laurens Johannes Griessel-Landau attempted to victimize Presley.

The doctor wormed his way into caring for the King's skin after sending a note of concern to the singer's secretary while Elvis was stationed in Germany with the U.S. Army. The dermatologist wrote, "I would not like to see him grow older. I clearly noticed the wrinkles on Mr. Presley's forehead." The note struck a chord with Elvis, and Dr. Griessel-Landau was soon hired to treat Elvis for crow's-feet, wrinkles, and other blemishes that had sprung up near his eyes and on his shoulders.

However, according to the FBI, Presley became impatient when the doctor began to make "improper [homosexual] advances" on his army buddies. When Elvis severed the relationship, Griessel-Landau got mad. He threatened to get back at Elvis by exposing his relationship with then sixteen-year-old Priscilla Beaulieu. The devious dermatologist even promised to release photos and tape recordings of Elvis in "compromising situations." The twisted matter eventually fizzled.

According to the FBI file at the time, "Presley assures us this [embarrassing photos of him and Priscilla] is impossible since he was never in any compromising situations."

A Lover and a Fighter

Many red-blooded American males despised the gyrating singer because their girlfriends became all shook up whenever they heard or saw Elvis perform.

Sometimes the jealousy boiled over and Elvis found himself in a confrontation. However, the King wasn't one to back down from a fight. And more often than not, it was Elvis who rocked and rolled his way to victory.

29

An unemployed steelworker named Louis John Balint took a poke at Elvis while the young star was visiting Toledo, Ohio, in 1956. Balint sucker-punched Presley at the posh Commodore Perry Hotel where Elvis was staying while in town for a show. Presley, who was stunned but not hurt by the blow, responded with a punch of his own. The angry assailant blamed Elvis for breaking up his marriage, even though the singer didn't know either Balint or his estranged wife.

When Balint was arrested, he told police his wife's love for Elvis was too much for him to bear. A judge couldn't bear Balint's tale of woe and socked him with a $19.60 fine for his unprovoked punch. The out-of-work defendant didn't have the money to pay for his crime, so he was sent to jail.

* * *

A month earlier, the King pulled into a Memphis service station and triggered a near riot when fans recognized his shiny Cadillac parked along the gas pumps.

Station manager Ed Hopper didn't appreciate the fact that the commotion meant lost business because, thanks to Elvis, no other paying customers could get their cars up to his pumps. Angry Ed first asked the singer to move along and take the mob with him. The miffed manager then made the mistake of slapping Elvis on the back of the head to better drive home his point. Elvis responded in kind with a quick punch to Ed's face.

When a second attendant—six-foot-four Aubrey Brown—entered the fray, he too got a Presley punch for his troubles. All three were arrested and charged with assault and battery. The next day, Elvis successfully defended himself in front of acting city judge Sam Friedman, who found Elvis innocent of any wrongdoing.

The attendants weren't as lucky. Hopper and Brown were each found guilty and fined twenty-five dollars.

"I'll take ridicule and slander," Presley told reporters afterward, "but when a guy hits me, that's too much."

* * *

Talk about knockout performances. A 1973 appearance by Elvis at the Las Vegas Hilton was disrupted by four drunken men who leaped onto the stage in the middle of his act and threatened to pummel the momentarily stunned singer.

While several Presley bodyguards easily handled three of the sauced assailants, Elvis disposed of the fourth man by slugging him hard enough to send him sprawling back into the crowd. The decked show-crasher landed in a heap after dive-bombing into a table filled with drinks.

As the four men were hustled out of the lounge, Elvis told the shocked crowd, "You'll have to excuse me. I would have beaten those guys up, but there were only four of them." The appreciative audience gave Elvis a seven-minute standing ovation for his one-punch knockout.

The foursome—Kenneth MacKenzie Jr., Roberto MacKenzie, Mario Martinez, and Marcello Jose Filas—continued their fight with Elvis, only this time in court. The men filed a four million-dollar lawsuit, claiming Elvis and a bunch of his friends attacked them. However, attorney Ronald Dwyer successfully defended his celebrity client, and the case was tossed out by superior court judge Robert Weil.

Temperature Rising

Elvis was a pacifist by nature, but according to those close to him, he possessed a hot temper.

Loew's State Theater in Memphis was the site of his first major blowup as a teen. Prior to his big break in music, schoolboy Elvis ushered at the cinema from five to ten P.M. weeknights for five weeks in 1952. He took home $12.75 a week and enjoyed plenty of free candy and popcorn from the pretty girl behind the concession counter, even though all employees were supposed to pay for their goodies. The freebies—and Elvis's job—ended when a fellow usher squealed on him.

It wasn't the sampling of sweets that led to Presley's dismissal. It was the fistfight that he engaged in with the tattler after Elvis learned he'd been fingered. Theater manager Arthur Groom lowered the boom and fired both ushers for the fisticuffs.

* * *

Years later, Presley's personal assistant, Alan Fortas, had a firsthand look at the sometimes violent mood swings of his boss. One night during a disagreement with friend and bodyguard Sonny West, Elvis hauled off and socked him on the jaw. Stunned Sonny had tears in his eyes as he asked, "Man, I can't believe you did that!"

Sonny was fired on the spot. But as was often the case, Elvis cooled off and rehired the bounced employee.

* * *

Author Christina Crawford, daughter of legendary actress Joan Crawford, triggered an Elvis outburst when she dared disagree with him at his home in 1974. According to Fortas, Elvis flew into a fit of rage, grabbed Crawford by the hair, dragged her across a marble coffee table, and pushed her off into another room to read her the riot act. The angry host allegedly gave his guest a few swift kicks in the butt for good measure, then showed her the door.

* * *

Once, while stopped at a red light in Los Angeles, Elvis was signing his autograph for a female driver who had stepped out of her car. When the light turned green, the driver in the car behind Presley started honking his horn obnoxiously.

"We were just driving down the street after that," recalled Presley's stepbrother David Stanley, "and that same car came up to us and tried to run us off the road. Several teenagers leaned out the car and yelled obscenities at us.

"Elvis was so ticked he grabbed his gun, rolled down the window, and yelled, 'Pull over! Pull over right now!' He pumped three shots into the air. They pulled up at the next light and we got out with our guns drawn. As soon as they recognized Elvis, they said, 'God, Elvis, we didn't know it was you. We're sorry.' So Elvis put his gun back into his pocket. He said, 'You've got no right to go around acting that way!' He gave them a good tongue-lashing before letting them go."

* * *

Elvis didn't look for fights, but when one arose, he didn't back down from anyone. The flashy singer was once cruising Los Angeles in a Cadillac convertible when a tough guy saluted him with an obscene gesture. Elvis caught sight of the finger-flicker, quickly slammed on the brakes of his Caddy, and made a sharp U-turn.

The incensed singer sped into the service station where the bird man stood with a bunch of his equally nasty-looking friends. In a flash, Elvis was out of the car and standing face-to-face with the grinning culprit. It didn't matter to the angry entertainer that there was a gang hanging around. Elvis strode up to the man who'd done the dirty deed and asked him face-to-face, "Did you shoot me the bird, buddy? I don't like people talking to me that way."

The offender lunged forward and took a swing. Elvis dodged the flying fist and let loose with a couple of lightning quick karate kicks that dropped the punk to the ground. No other gang member made a move as Elvis calmly collected himself, headed back to his car, and drove away.

"I'm a lover, not a fighter."

The Country Boy
Serves His Country

Operation Elvis

Elvis was at the peak of popularity when he received his draft notice on December 10, 1957. The army expected the singer to report for active duty a month later. However, that date conflicted with the filming of Presley's fourth movie, *King Creole,* so the wheels were quickly set in motion to stall his induction.

Paramount Studios production chief Frank Freeman sent an urgent request for a sixty-day postponement that would allow the army-bound actor enough time to complete his film. The draft board notified Freeman that such a request must come from the recruit himself. Elvis eagerly followed up with a similar plea and was given a sixty-day deferment.

Even though the deferment was only for two months, it so enraged Kentucky state representative Nick Johnson that he resigned from his position on the draft board. The native of Harlan, Kentucky, declared, "I cannot conscientiously ask any mountain boy to serve the same country unless afforded the same treatment as Presley."

Following a whirlwind shooting schedule, Elvis finally reported for active duty at Fort Chaffee, Arkansas, on March 25, 1958.

* * *

The man who inducted Elvis into the army in 1958 very nearly ended up as his father-in-law in 1977. Sgt. Walter Alden never dreamed the raw-boned recruit from Memphis would one day be engaged to his daughter Ginger. After all, Miss Alden was all of two years old at the time!

But young Ginger eventually blossomed into a shapely beauty who would become the King's last girlfriend. Ginger had the dubious distinction of sharing Elvis's bed the day he died at Graceland.

* * *

After completing basic training, Presley was given orders to report to Germany.

The Military Ocean Terminal in Brooklyn was the point of embarkation for Elvis on September 22, 1958. A huge crowd gathered to wish the singer bon voyage. An army band launched Presley into his new career with rousing military versions of "All Shook Up," "Hound Dog," "Don't Be Cruel," "Tutti Frutti," "Dixie," and "Sentimental Journey."

The last American to kiss Elvis before he headed to Germany to begin serving Uncle Sam was model Lillian Portnoy. There were no complaints from the recruit as lovely Lillian offered him a cheesecake and a buss on the lips moments before he boarded the USS *Randall*.

* * *

The Pentagon pressured Elvis to become part of the Army Special Services so he could entertain the troops. But such an assignment rankled Col. Tom Parker. The money-minded manager certainly didn't want his client performing for free while in the army, so he insisted Elvis be treated just like any other soldier.

Parker was so adamant that Presley not perform for the army that he flew to Washington, D.C., to speak directly with Lt. Gen. William H. Arnold, the commander of the Fifth Army.

Soon, Elvis was an ordinary member of A Company, Second Medium Tank Battalion, Second Armored Division in Wiesbaden, Germany.

* * *

Elvis didn't ask for any special favors while in the army. He gladly accepted his job as a Jeep driver and was one of only five soldiers to get a perfect rating for vehicle maintenance. His comrades in arms said it wasn't uncommon for Elvis to get down on his hands and knees to sandpaper the exhaust pipe until it shined.

The army helped Elvis develop into a great marksman. In fact, he was awarded three medals for marksmanship with his rifle, pistol, and carbine rifle.

* * *

While on weekend leave from the army in Germany in June 1959, Elvis dropped an estimated $10,000 so he could live it up with some pals in Paris. Elvis had chartered a plane to whisk his companions from Germany to France.

Joining Elvis for the boys' night out were Charlie Hodge, Rex Mansfield, and Lamar Fike. Upon arriving in Paris, Elvis discovered he'd left his army hat back at the German base. He simply put Fike back on the plane and had his pal retrieve it for him!

While at the Lido nightclub, Private Presley entertained the crowd by playing the piano and singing "Willow Weep for Me."

The fun-seeking foursome went club hopping at places such as the Folies-Bergère, the Café de Paris, the Carousel, the Moulin Rouge, and the 4 O'Clock Club. Elvis and the boys picked up the entire Blue Bell chorus line at the 4 O'Clock Club and invited them back to their hotel for a late-night party. The partygoers rode from place to place in style— in a flashy Cadillac limousine that cost Elvis eight hundred dollars to rent.

* * *

Unfortunately, Elvis's first exposure to drugs occurred while he served in the army. The young recruit, and others serving as overnight sentries, were reportedly given Dexedrine pills to help keep them awake and alert during guard duty.

* * *

Elvis had been raking in a cool $400,000 a month before Uncle Sam came calling. Once he was drafted, the U.S. government began paying the singing soldier boy the standard buck private pay of seventy-eight dollars a month.

While young Elvis fulfilled his army requirements, the federal government lost out on tens of thousands of dollars that the IRS would have collected on Presley's income had he been performing.

* * *

Elvis was such a great fan of the military that he took it upon himself to learn Gen. Douglas MacArthur's farewell speech word for word. Later in life, the singer would inspire his employees with quotes from the stirring speech.

* * *

By the time he was discharged, Elvis had attained the rank of sergeant. But that rank wasn't good enough for him. The creative soldier gave himself a "promotion" by simply having an extra stripe sewn onto his custom-made uniform. That extra touch made Elvis a staff sergeant—but in his own mind only.

Elvis and the FBI

Ironically, even though the FBI kept a huge file on Elvis, the King went to FBI headquarters and volunteered to act as an informant for the bureau. Presley told authorities he was willing to spy on those in the entertainment world who were critical of the government or involved in drugs.

In 1970, Elvis pushed for a meeting with his hero—FBI chief J. Edgar Hoover. The encounter almost became a reality until worried FBI aides stepped in. The squeaky-clean underlings despised the long hair and outrageous clothing sported by Elvis and suggested Hoover take evasive action.

An internal FBI memo by agent M.A. Jones acknowledged that Presley "was interested in becoming active in the drive against the use of narcotics, particularly by young people." But the memo concluded that Hoover should turn down Presley's request for a meeting: "It is noted at the present time he [Elvis] is wearing his hair down to his shoulders and indulges in the wearing of all sorts of exotic dress. Presley's sincerity and good intentions notwithstanding, he is certainly not the type of individual whom the director would wish to meet." A Hoover aide attached a picture of Elvis shaking hands with President Richard Nixon to illustrate the odd attire of the singer.

It would have been a dream come true for Elvis to meet the larger-than-life man behind the FBI. Despite a letter of introduction from Senator George Murphy—a former movie actor—the meeting never took place. The wary Hoover accepted the advice of his worried aides and was conveniently "out of town" the day Elvis came calling at the FBI's Washington-based headquarters. Nevertheless, Presley was given a tour of the place by an official.

After Presley's visit, a memo noted that "in his [Elvis's] opinion, no one has ever done as much for his country as has Mr. Hoover, and that he, Presley, considers the Director the 'greatest living American.' "

According to the report, Elvis "is of the opinion that the Beatles laid the groundwork for many of the problems we are having with young people by their filthy unkempt appearance and suggestive music. . . ." He advised that the Smothers Brothers, Jane Fonda, and others in the entertainment industry of their ilk have a lot to answer for in the hereafter for the way they have poisoned young minds by disparaging the United States in their public statements and unsavory activities.

"Presley privately advised that he has volunteered his services to the President in connection with the narcotics problem and that Mr. Nixon had responded by furnishing him with an agent's badge of the Bureau of Narcotics and Dangerous Drugs. Presley was carrying the badge in his pocket and displayed it."

The FBI report made special mention of Presley's willingness to act as an informant in the entertainment industry. The memo stated that Presley reported being approached by persons "whose motives and goals he is convinced are not in the best interest of this country and who seek to have him lend his name to their questionable activities. In this regard, he volunteered to make such information available to the bureau on a confidential basis whenever it came to his attention."

There was nothing in the FBI file that confirms any case in which Presley acted as an informant.

Elvis and the President

Elvis personally met with President Richard Nixon at the White House, where the singer revealed he had been studying Communist brainwashing techniques and vowed to support the president against the Red Menace.

The meeting took place on December 21, 1970, a few weeks before he visited the FBI. Presley got his audience with the president just a few hours after personally delivering to a White House guard a letter seeking such a meeting. The letter stated:

Dear Mr. President:

First, I would like to introduce myself. I am Elvis Presley and admire you and have Great Respect for your office. I talked to Vice President Spiro Agnew in Palm Springs three weeks ago and expressed my concern for our country. The Drug Culture, the Hippie elements, the S.D.S. (Students for a Democratic Society), Black Panthers, etc. do *not* consider me as their enemy or as they call it the Establishment. . . . I have no concerns or motives other than helping the country out. So I wish not to be given a title or an appointed position. I can and will do more good if I were made a Federal Agent at Large and I will help out by doing it through my communications with people of all ages.

Sir, I am staying at the Washington Hotel. . . . I am registered under the name of Jon Burrows. I will be here for as long as it takes to get the credentials of a Federal Agent. I have done an indepth study of drug abuse and Communist brainwashing techniques and I am right in the middle of the whole thing where I can and will do the most good.

I am glad to help just so long as it is kept very private. . . . I was nominated this coming year one of America's Ten Most Outstanding Young Men. . . . I am sending you the short autobiography about myself so you can better understand this approach. I would love to meet with you just to say hello if you're not too busy.

Respectfully,
Elvis Presley

The letter worked. Presley got his brief meeting with the president. After the meeting, White House aide Bud Krogh filed this memo:

The meeting opened with pictures taken of the President and Elvis Presley.

Presley immediately began showing the President his law enforcement badges from police departments in California, Colorado, and Tennessee. . . .

The President mentioned that he thought Presley could reach young people, and that it was important for Presley to retain his credibility. Presley responded that he did his thing by "just singing.". . .

Presley indicated that he thought the Beatles had been a real force for anti-American spirit. He said that the Beatles came to this country, made their money, and then returned to England where they promoted an anti-American theme. The President nodded in agreement and expressed some surprise. The President then indicated that those who use drugs are also those in the vanguard of anti-American protest. . . . Presley indicated to the President in a very emotional manner that he was "on your side.". . . He also mentioned that he had been studying Communist brainwashing and the drug culture for over 10 years. He mentioned he knew a lot about this and was accepted by the Hippies. . . . At the conclusion of the meeting, Presley again told the President how much he supported him, and then, in a surprising, spontaneous gesture, put his left arm around the President and hugged him. . . .

Presley received an honorary Narcotics Bureau badge and then presented Nixon with a gift. In a note days later, the President thanked Presley for his "thoughtfulness in giving me the commemorative World War II Colt .45 pistol, encased in the handsome wooden chest."

* * *

The Narcotics Bureau badge was one of Presley's favorite possessions, which is ironic since the singer's death was linked to his staggering abuse of prescription drugs.

Weeks before Presley received the badge, Narcotics Bureau head John Finlater rejected Elvis's original request for one, even after Presley offered a contribution of $50,000 to the antidrug campaign. So Elvis decided to go over Finlater's head to the President himself, who got the honorary badge from Finlater.

"I love this country and what it stands for. These war protesters should go live somewhere else, along with any others who don't care to stand up for their country."

Boys Will Be Boys

Letting His Hair Down

    Elvis loved to play the bigshot when it came to having fun.

    For years, Presley would entertain his pals at the Fairgrounds Amusement Park in Memphis. When in town, Elvis often rented the entire park for his personal amusement. The singer sometimes let the public join in the fun even though fair officials closed the park when Elvis arrived.

    The Memphis hepcat didn't think twice about gathering a rowdy bunch and converging on the amusement park during the early morning hours. Elvis would plunk down $2,500 just so he and his pals could enjoy the stomach-flipping rides.

    The King was in control of the rides—and everyone else was at his mercy. Woozy passengers would find themselves traveling the roller coaster route as many as twenty straight times before Elvis finally tired of the dips and twists and brought the ride to a welcome stop. Then he would lead everyone to the Dodgem Cars, where he proceeded to bash into everyone's car again and again.

The last time Elvis rented the amusement park was August 8, 1977—just a week before his death. From 1:15 A.M. until dawn, Elvis, his daughter Lisa Marie, his girlfriend Ginger Alden, and a dozen friends enjoyed the rides.

* * *

A lot cheaper to rent was the Rainbow Rollerdome in Memphis. Elvis needed just seventy dollars for a night of thrills and spills. He and his guests often got into some rough roller-skating games. Pretty soon, participants took to donning elbow and knee pads to help soften the blows when they fell on the hard wooden floor.

* * *

Presley also enjoyed football, and on many occasions he'd round up his buddies, rent the Whitehaven High School stadium in Memphis, and hire an official for an afternoon of pigskin action. Elvis often played end for his team. Later, the singer equipped the players with snazzy uniforms.

Presley was an avid fan of the Cleveland Browns. In fact, he claimed he could name all the members of the Browns and many of the players on the other NFL teams too.

* * *

Presley used to have races with his friends in souped up go-carts that zoomed around the Graceland grounds at speeds of up to seventy miles an hour.

Elvis also loved the thrill of speeding down the road on his motorcycle. Recalled his stepbrother Billy Stanley, "We'd be going down the expressway at 120 miles an hour, and that's pretty damn fast for two wheels. Elvis would take his hands off the handle bars—doing 120—and start flapping his arms up and down real slow like a bird. If you were behind him, it looked like he was flying."

Pajama Games

Prior to entering the army, the nineteen-year-old singer developed a bizarre relationship with a trio of thirteen-year-old girls. There was nothing sexual about the King's fling with Gloria, Heidi, and Frances, according to his true-blue employees. The get-togethers may sound kinky in this day and age, but for Elvis they were a way of staying young at heart. At least, that's the claim of insiders who explain that Elvis was simply behaving like a boy trapped in the body of a man.

The giggling teens spent hours at Graceland engaging in childish antics like watermelon seed-spitting contests, pillow fights, tickling, rolling on his oversized bed, and tossing each other into the pool. Elvis enjoyed playing the part of a fourteen-year-old boy rather than a budding man and always backed off if his young guests complained he was going "too far."

The foursome organized wacky pajama parties where Elvis allowed his special guests to wash and dry his hair. In exchange for such pampering, Elvis would apply eye shadow and makeup to his junior-high honeys.

When it was time to call it a night, the gracious host would click off the light and lie down with one girl nestled in each arm and the third draped across his feet. The trusting teens didn't spend the entire night at Graceland. They'd be escorted home to their respective parents in the wee hours of the morning.

* * *

The little kid inside the big star revealed himself when Memphis was socked in by a blizzard in the early 1960s. Schools, roads, and public buildings may have been closed, but Graceland was open for fun. Elvis bundled up like an Eskimo and had his limo driver head out to round up friends and relatives for three days of frolicking in the sixteen-inch snow.

Ever since his widowed father married Dee Stanley about a year after Gladys's death, Presley had become extremely fond of his younger stepbrothers David, Billy, and Rick Stanley. So on the day of the big snow, he decided to share some winter fun with them.

The boys were sitting down for breakfast when a limo pulled up and the driver began shoveling a path to the front door of their house. Minutes later, Elvis got out of the car and announced there was no time to waste. The Stanley brothers piled into the limo and made their way slowly back to Elvis's mansion. The next few days were filled with snowball fights, sledding, and snowmobile riding on the spacious grounds.

A Blast from the Past

Elvis was addicted to fireworks.

He couldn't get enough of them. From the time his career began to skyrocket, Presley was firing off everything from bottle rockets to large, dangerous pyrotechnics.

While traveling by car from gig to gig in the early days, Elvis literally had a blast tossing firecrackers at roadside targets. Drummer D.J. Fontana recalled how the trips took longer than they should have because Elvis was always insisting they stop for more firecrackers.

The more money Presley made, the more he spent on fireworks. Elvis would routinely plunk down thousands of dollars for an explosive array of pyrotechnics on the usual occasions like the Fourth of July or New Year's Eve.

But there were also bang-up special days when Elvis and his buddies conducted wild war games. The weapons of choice were buzz bombs, sky rockets, Roman candles—just about anything that they could launch at one another. The louder the better, too. The opposing armies would dress in flight suits, gloves, racing goggles, and rags to cover their faces from the ashes and burning fallout of the fireworks.

In *Life With Elvis,* stepbrother David Stanley said that in looking back at these explosive encounters, he wonders how the soldiers escaped with their lives. "We would take huge fireworks meant for aerial displays and shoot them at one another," wrote Stanley. "If you ever got hit by one of those things, you knew it. It's a wonder that we didn't have any serious injuries, but we never did."

Elvis got a kick out of taking an entire twelve-pack of Roman candles and lighting them all at once. He'd then run off like a madman, all the while shooting the fire balls at his enemies. On one wild Fourth of July, combatant Richard Davis, a Graceland employee, took a direct hit to the face from a buzz bomb. He fell like a ton of bricks and an immediate truce was called so his condition could be checked. The heat from the buzz bomb had melted the plastic on Richard's goggles, but he escaped any serious injury from the friendly fire. Despite the scare, Elvis and his buddies were back at war just moments after Richard left for a hospital checkup.

Another time, during one of these "wars," an errant rocket landed in the large Graceland carport where Elvis stored his explosives, and a fire broke out. For a frightening twenty minutes, the warriors were glued to the ground in order to escape the whizzing fireworks that flew wildly by, just inches above their heads. The local fire department arrived at the scene, but firefighters had to find cover until the last explosive had detonated.

The shelling of Graceland almost cost Elvis some of his favorite automobiles. His Ferraris, Cadillacs, and other fancy vehicles in the carport suffered burn damage from the out-of-control fireworks, but fortunately the hot cars escaped any serious damage.

The Graceland Zoo

Elvis loved animals and practically transformed the grounds of Graceland into a wildlife refuge. Dogs, horses, monkeys, chimpanzees, peacocks, mules, and a herd of other animals wandered the spacious estate.

Presley's most incorrigible pet was a chimpanzee named Scatter. Elvis and his buddies thought it was a hoot to teach Scatter bad habits like sitting on a bar stool and drinking bourbon or harassing unsuspecting women by tugging on their skirts and pinching their bottoms.

Scatter had free run of Graceland until he began acting a bit too violently and had to be locked away. Before that though, the booze-swilling chimp would sit at the dinner table and eat with a knife and fork. He was even chauffeured around in the back of a Rolls or Cadillac.

One Christmas, Dee Presley thought Scatter would look nice in a little sport coat. But the naughty chimp felt differently about his natty attire. As Dee tried to dress Scatter, he grabbed her hand, stuck it in his mouth, and started biting down hard. "I started screaming, but Vernon and Elvis were falling on the floor laughing because they thought I was laughing!" Dee recalled. There was nothing funny about Dee's trip to the hospital to have her hand treated.

The laughs began to fade as Scatter aged into an uncontrollable nuisance who terrorized guests at Graceland. Eventually Scatter had to be confined to a cage, where the cantankerous chimp was well cared for until his death from cirrhosis of the liver.

* * *

One of Presley's favorite dogs was a chow chow named Getlo. When the dog became sick with a kidney disease, Elvis spared no expense. He flew the canine to Boston so a prominent physician—not a veterinarian—could treat him. But despite the pricey medical care, the dog died. It took Elvis weeks to get over the loss.

* * *

Two of Elvis's dogs were in the movies with him. A collie named Baba made a cameo appearance in Presley's 1966 movie *Paradise Hawaiian Style*. Two years later, in the movie *Live a Little, Love a Little*, his Great Dane Brutus played the part of a dog named Albert.

Among other dogs, Presley also had poodles named Hugo, Samson, and Teddy Bear of Zizipompom.

* * *

Elvis loved riding horses. Graceland had a stable which he remodeled and equipped with a stall for each steed. At one time, he owned over a dozen thoroughbreds.

The stable was named the House of the Rising Sun in honor of his favorite mount, Rising Sun. Among his other horses were Domino, Colonel Midnight, Lady, Golden Sun, Scout, Flaming Star, Sheba, Thundercloud, El Poco, Beauty, Traveler, Bear, Keno, Buckshot, Sun Down, Star Trek, and Big Red. Presley named another one of his horses Mare Ingram after Memphis mayor William Ingram.

* * *

Before it had water, the lavish Graceland swimming pool was once the home of four donkeys. The four asses—a gift from Colonel Parker—were temporarily housed in the empty pool until a more fitting home could be found.

* * *

Elvis spoiled the animals and let them have the run of the estate—even when it proved costly.

In 1961, Presley signed a lucrative movie contract, so he celebrated by buying a new Rolls-Royce Phantom V. But when he brought it home to Graceland, the pet peacocks, chickens, and a turkey named Bow Tie pecked away at their reflections in the finish of the shiny new car.

While many of the household staff wanted to get rid of the birds, Elvis refused because they had been the pets of his late mother Gladys. Instead, he had the badly pecked car repainted several times.

Food for Thought

Perhaps it was the fact that his family had to scrimp that led Elvis to his amazing obsession for food. The singer loved king-size portions of the most unhealthy dishes. His last meal was four scoops of ice cream and eight cookies.

That wasn't even close to his usual standards of snacking gluttony—at least eight scoops of ice cream and two dozen cookies in one sitting.

* * *

Elvis seemed to associate bad foods with good times. Skippy peanut butter was a childhood favorite of his—and comprised many a meal for the struggling Presley family. When company would arrive at his small Tupelo home, Elvis would often grab the jar of peanut butter and hide it out of fear it would be eaten by the guests.

* * *

Elvis liked his food well done. Whether it was bacon, eggs, burgers, or steaks, the King ate it charred. He often sent platters back to the kitchen so the food could be burned a bit more. A bowl filled with supercrispy bacon was a frequent companion by his home piano.

But Presley's favorite food was pork chops smothered in brown gravy and served with apple pie for dessert.

* * *

Once Elvis began making money, he indulged in one of his great passions—eating junk food. On the road, he would consume as many as eight cheeseburgers and three milk shakes at a sitting. At home, he loved to munch on a sandwich of peanut butter, sliced bananas, and crisp bacon.

He had cooks on call twenty-four hours a day at Graceland to make him whatever he wanted whenever he wanted it.

* * *

The house drink at Graceland was Pepsi. Elvis sucked down so much of the cola that a local distributor made Graceland one of its regular stops.

* * *

Elvis and some of his ever-present pals were sitting around one February night in 1976 when the King got the craving for the artery-clogging concoction called the Fool's Gold Loaf. No matter that the sandwich was the specialty of a Denver restaurant and the entertainer was in Memphis at the time. The King had the order placed, and within minutes he and his crew were zooming by private jet to Colorado.

There they dined on the still-warm sandwiches made from an entire hollowed-out whole loaf of bread that was spread with a generous portion of peanut butter and jelly and filled with a fat-soaked pound of crispy fried bacon.

* * *

Elvis was known to eat hot fudge sundaes for breakfast. One time, before a concert in Baltimore, he reportedly wolfed down five sundaes for breakfast and then passed out.

* * *

In his book *The Life and Cuisine of Elvis Presley*, author David Adler claims that near the end of his life, Elvis often ate while reclining. Because it was impossible to eat and watch TV while lying flat in bed, Elvis wore a pair of glasses with a mirror inside. Positioned at a forty-five-degree angle, the mirror reflected the TV sets that were at the foot of his bed so he could see them while stretched out.

According to Adler, Presley favored one meal in his final days—bacon, mashed potatoes, and crowder peas, which he swirled around together on his plate and shoveled in his mouth with his bare hands.

Elvis's Gold Car

Elvis loved cars and bought dozens upon dozens of them.

He may have attained his golden moment of glitz when he had a 1960 Cadillac done over and accessorized by Barris Custom City of North Hollywood. By the time the work was done, the vehicle was almost as golden as a Presley hit record.

George Barris—the king of car customizers—took the Series 75 Sedan Limousine and transformed it into the famous gorgeous gold Cadillac.

The $100,000 Caddy had an exterior coated with a glistening gold and diamond-flake paint job. In all, there were forty layers of the hand-rubbed glitter paint that also included Oriental fish scales to give it an extra sparkle.

Passengers in the gold Cadillac were hidden from the gawking public by gold lamé curtains. The impressive auto was full of fourteen-karat accessories. It featured gold-plated bumpers and hand-spun gold hubcaps, an electric razor, shoe buffer, bar, record player, and swivel TV—all solid gold. Alas, its two telephones were gold plated.

Even Elvis knew his special car was impractical. After all, he couldn't drive it any-where without attracting a mob, and the Caddy couldn't be parked without someone standing guard over it. The golden chariot soon was banished to a Graceland garage until Col. Tom Parker came up with the bright idea to put the Elvis car on tour while its busy owner was working on an acting career.

Crafty Parker knew a money-maker when he saw one. He talked RCA into buying the car for $24,000 and sending it on the road to promote the new Elvis flick *Frankie and Johnny*. There were plenty of stops along the way at shopping centers and movie theater parking lots. Of course, souvenir postcards of the car were available.

The expensive vehicle was towed from city to city, where young and old alike lined up to get a close look at Elvis's goldmobile. The car eventually made its way to the Country Music Hall of Fame in Nashville.

"There's no such thing as a man...
just a little boy wearin' a man's body."

Number One— With a Bullet

Pistol-Packin' Presley

Elvis was a trigger-happy star who often acted like he was living in the Wild West. In fact, he endangered the lives of his family and friends with his reckless disregard for gun safety.

Presley usually packed at least one pistol on him when he ventured beyond the safety of his Graceland gates. While Elvis had a blast toying around with his fancy cars, he really got a bang out of his amazing arsenal of firearms. He loved to shoot at things as he roared by on country roads. He often engaged in target practice in the backyard of Graceland. He would shoot heavy weaponry, like .357 magnums, Thompson submachine guns, and even army-issue M-16 automatic rifles.

During his later years, Elvis combined his affection for firearms with his addiction to drugs. That lethal combination nearly led to the death of his personal physician, Dr. George Nichopoulos.

"Dr. Nick" regularly doled out prescription drugs for his patient. On one occasion, while on tour, Elvis came back from a dental visit with a smorgasbord of free drug samples. That didn't sit well with Dr. Nick, who confiscated the extra drugs. But like a kid whose candy was taken away from him, Elvis responded with anger.

The peeved singer summoned Dr. Nick to his backstage suite, where the physician plopped down on a couch next to Elvis's father, Vernon. Things proceeded to get a bit crazy when Elvis pulled out one of his many handguns and began waving it around. He calmly told the now nervous doctor that he needed his pills back. When Dr. Nick adamantly refused, Elvis took aim at a leg of the couch and pulled the trigger. The bullet bounced off the hard wood and began ricocheting around the small room. The spent slug came to a sickening stop when it smacked the doctor square in the chest! Luckily, by that time there wasn't enough force behind the bullet to do any physical harm.

"The singer laughed and treated it like a joke," according to Dennis Breo, author of *Extraordinary Care*. "Vernon Presley was quiet as Dr. Nick told his patient, 'Elvis, you're displaying some pretty poor judgment. You know your daddy just had a heart attack and he can do without this kind of nonsense. And so can I.'"

At that point, the band struck up the music to alert Elvis it was time to head for the stage. He calmly put down the gun and went out to face his screaming fans. After the show, the angry doctor chewed out his patient once again. Unfortunately, neither Dr. Nick nor anyone else could stop the drug-induced downward spiral that would eventually spell doom for Elvis.

Presley's love for guns far exceeded his concern for safety. Some of his other shocking shooting incidents include:

* Narrowly missing accidentally killing girlfriend Linda Thompson with a .22 caliber slug. Elvis had casually fired his gun at a light switch in an adjoining room of his Las Vegas hotel suite in 1974. The bullet went through the wall and into the bathroom where Linda was taking a shower.

* Blasting his Ferrari with two pistol loads of bullets after its drained battery failed to start the sports car.

* Destroying a lavish chandelier at the Imperial Suite at the Las Vegas Hilton with several shots from a handgun. Elvis then egged his entourage into joining him in "light" target practice.

* Blowing a hole in the ceiling of a restaurant because the table service was too slow for his taste.

* Firing a shot at the ceiling of a penthouse. Presley casually told his stunned friends, "If this is really the penthouse, there ain't nothin' above us that could get hurt."

* Shooting up his personal recording studio at Graceland. Elvis didn't like the sound he'd produced so he pulled out a pistol and began blazing away at the speakers.

Muzak to His Ears

Singer Robert Goulet was an instant target when Elvis saw him on TV. It didn't matter where the gun-slinging Presley was—at home or in a hotel. If he saw Goulet singing on television, Elvis would whip out his .357 magnum or whatever else was handy and blast the television screen.

Presley hated Goulet's singing because the King believed Goulet was all technique and no feeling.

Jazz singer Mel Torme also ticked off Elvis for the same reason. The Velvet Fog sounded more like a frog to the unappreciative Presley—and the end result was usually another TV destroyed by a bullet from Elvis's gun.

Triggering a Shopping Spree

Business was booming at Kerr's Sporting Goods store in Beverly Hills where Elvis spent $38,000 on guns in one day in 1970. Among the pricier handguns were a $1,900 .357 Colt Python and a $1,800 .44 Ruger Black Hawk. Two years later, Elvis came back to Kerr's to buy even more firepower.

At the time of his death, Elvis owned thirty-seven hand-guns, rifles, and machine guns—and one sawed-off shotgun.

* * *

Elvis carried a special gun to the movie theater a week before he died.

Presley had rented an entire theater in Memphis so he and his pals could watch a private midnight screening of the James Bond flick *The Spy Who Loved Me*. Elvis brought along his PPK Walther pistol—because that's the model agent 007 used to blast the bad guys.

Deputy Presley

On September 1, 1970, Elvis was sworn in as a special deputy of Shelby County, Tennessee. Sheriff Roy Nixon conducted the ceremony as a favor for Elvis after the singer made it known he wanted to carry a weapon for defense against his crazier fans.

Tennessee state law prohibited private citizens from packing heat, so Sheriff Nixon came to the rescue, proclaiming Elvis one of his special officers. Deputy Presley now had the right to carry a concealed weapon—and he often took advantage of it. The gun-toting deputy was deadly serious about treating his position with respect—and action.

Elvis loved to "patrol" the highways of Shelby County. Often he'd slap a blue light on top of his speedy black Ferrari and go in search of lawbreakers. When he spotted an obvious speeder, the King of the Road would flick on the flashing light and take off in pursuit.

The speeder would get the shock of his life when Elvis strolled up to his window and

announced: "Excuse me, but you were going pretty fast, sir. I think you'd better slow it down a little bit."

Out-of-staters got a different sermon from Deputy Presley: "We have laws around here that we're pretty particular about. And the speed limit is one of these laws. We'd appreciate it if you'd slow it down a little bit." Then in a flash, the supercop celebrity was gone in search of other speeders.

* * *

Elvis was so obsessed with law enforcement that he became friends with police officers everywhere. In Denver, he held the honorary rank of captain. When one of his law enforcement friends died, Elvis showed up at the funeral in full uniform.

In 1956, he was bestowed the honorary title of captain of the Louisiana State Highway Patrol. The award included another badge for the Presley collection.

Hit Maker to Hit Man

Elvis hatched a plot to personally murder several drug dealers in Memphis.

Presley was so motivated by the bloody Charles Bronson action film *Death Wish* that he wanted to mimic its violent vigilante premise. After seeing the movie, Elvis returned to Graceland and began planning the demise of the Memphis drug dealers who'd allegedly hooked his stepbrother Ricky Stanley on heroin.

Boyhood friends turned bodyguards Red and Sonny West were summoned to a room that Elvis had transformed into an impressive arsenal of weaponry. There were at least a dozen rifles, two dozen pistols, several automatic weapons, machine guns, rocket launchers, and piles of ammunition in view as the stunned Wests walked in.

Elvis figured his impressive cache of weapons could wipe out the men responsible for the drug problems in his favorite city. The singer even handed Red an envelope that contained the photographs and names of the suspected sleazeballs he wanted to put out of business for good.

Insiders said Memphis police provided Elvis with the information on the drug dealers. The warped plan called for several of Presley's bodyguards to lure the drug dealers into an ambush. Elvis himself would pull the trigger. The singer even arranged for a recording studio alibi in case police investigators came calling.

Presley's plot was never carried out, and the Memphis massacre was averted.

"[Shooting] is a challenge, an outlet...
and a way of staying alive."

Leading Ladies

That's All Right (Mama)

Elvis always had a strong psychic and emotional bond with his beloved mother, Gladys.

Once in 1954, Presley and his band mates were traveling to their gigs around the South in a 1954 Cadillac when the car caught fire and burned near Texarkana, Arkansas. Miles away in Memphis, Gladys was asleep at the time of the late-night incident when she had a disturbing dream. At the very moment the pink Cadillac burst into flames, Gladys awoke from a sound sleep and cried out her son's name. In her dream, she had seen her son surrounded by fire. Gladys discovered that it was much more than a bad dream when Elvis phoned home the next day to report the fiery mishap.

As an adult, Elvis was still so close to his mother that they would use baby talk when they conversed with each other. His vocabulary included words such as "toofies" for teeth, "sooties" for feet, "yittle" for little, and "yuv" for love. He liked to call her his "best girl."

Recalled his personal assistant, Alan Fortas, "Every time Elvis left the house with me or anyone else, Gladys would tell us, 'Take care of my baby.' And even if we only went to a movie, Elvis would call her at least a couple of times just to let her know he was all right."

Early in Presley's career, it took a while for Mama to get used to the fans' fawning over her only son. Gladys went wild when she watched a sea of screaming young girls fight for a piece of Elvis during a typically crazy Mississippi concert. Gladys jumped into the fray, grabbed hold of one out-of-control teen, and whirled her around. "Why are you trying to kill my boy?" she shouted.

The stress of such overwhelming adulation for her son eventually got to Gladys. She suffered from a drinking problem that only got worse and her health began to deteriorate. She died on August 14, 1958, from a liver ailment at the age of forty-six.

When Elvis got the phone call of her death, he rushed to the hospital. He and his father were heard wailing as they prayed over her body.

"She's all we lived for," Elvis told a reporter the next day.

Elvis was never the same after that fateful day. He went ballistic when his mama's body was taken to Graceland in a beautiful silver casket. She lay in state with the coffin lid open in the mansion. The distraught Elvis then grabbed her body and held it and kissed it, crying out for her to come back from the dead.

According to his aunt Lillian, "Elvis grabbed ahold of her pink housecoat—the one she wore all the time—and he went tearing up and down the stairs, hanging onto it and fondling it and kissing it. It was the most pitiful sight you ever saw."

At her graveside service, Elvis wailed: "Good-bye, darling, good-bye. I lived my whole life for you! Oh, God, everything I have is gone."

* * *

Mother and son maintained an almost unreal devotion to each other—one that carried over beyond the grave.

The sudden death of Gladys left a gaping hole in Presley's heart. But the singer always believed his mama's spirit was at his side at all times. In fact, the ghost of Gladys haunted—and by some accounts still haunts—the Graceland mansion. Elvis swore his mother would sometimes call out to him in the middle of the night. And he wasn't the only person to hear the haunting voice of Gladys.

One night during dinner at Graceland, Elvis and all his dinner guests heard a woman's voice call out his name. Bodyguards stood by Elvis with guns drawn while the others thoroughly searched the mansion from top to bottom. Nothing turned up, so Elvis turned in. But while he lay in bed that night, he heard the voice again—this time from the direction of the room that once belonged to his mother.

* * *

In March 1977, Elvis thought he'd found the reincarnation of his dear mother. While waiting for his car outside the gates of Graceland, a stunned Elvis spotted a female fan who, for some reason, he felt was spiritually linked to Gladys. Her name was Ellen Foster of St. Charles, Illinois.

Elvis invited the shocked fan into his Graceland home and spent some time chatting with her. Before releasing his special guest, Elvis presented her with a diamond ring. It was no ordinary ring. This was the diamond ring he'd given his mom in 1955. Ellen returned home a very happy woman and an even bigger Presley fan than she'd been before her lucky visit to Memphis.

Elvis and Priscilla

Priscilla Beaulieu was introduced to soldier boy Elvis when she was just fourteen years old while he was stationed in Germany.

Airman Currie Grant did the honors at the Presley family's rented house in Bad Nauheim. She wore a blue and white sailor-suit dress and white socks. Elvis called the pretty teenage army brat Cilla and convinced her to dye her hair black because he had liked the look on actress Debra Paget, who costarred in his 1956 flick *Love Me Tender*.

Elvis burned up the phone lines for a full year before convincing Priscilla's stepfather, Captain Joseph Beaulieu, to allow her to finish school in Memphis. The captain finally relented, and Priscilla moved into Graceland, under the watchful eye of Presley's family, and attended Immaculate Conception, an all-girls Catholic high school.

When she graduated, Elvis presented her with a new Corvair—the first of many cars that he gave to her. Elvis didn't attend Priscilla's 1963 graduation ceremony. He was well aware that his presence at the solemn proceedings would cause a major disturbance. So in order not to ruin the special day, Elvis sat outside in his car until Priscilla and her classmates were official grads.

After she turned twenty-one, Elvis proposed to her on Christmas Eve, 1966. They were married in a private ceremony in Las Vegas four months later.

* * *

Priscilla Beaulieu Presley became a model citizen while living in Memphis—literally.

At Elvis's urging, his lovely bride took several modeling courses at the Patricia Stevens Finishing School. Part of the program included lunchtime modeling shows at a local restaurant. Priscilla took part in the events under an assumed name, so many diners didn't digest the fact they were gazing upon Mrs. Elvis Presley.

Heir to the Throne

The birth of Elvis's daughter Lisa Marie went off without a hitch on February 1, 1968. But the events leading up to the blessed moment read like something out of a spy novel.

Presley and his entourage developed an elaborate plan to keep the prying press off their trail when the time came for Priscilla to give birth. Since nosy newsmen often camped outside the gates of Graceland, Elvis decided to trick them so they wouldn't follow him to the hospital. He had several decoy cars dispatched to lure them away.

Priscilla and Elvis climbed into the backseat of one of his new Cadillacs driven by buddy Charlie Hodge. A second Cadillac followed just in case the first car broke down en route to the hospital.

However, Hodge fouled up the four-mile drive when he headed for the wrong hospital. He had forgotten the plans had been changed to use Baptist Hospital instead of Methodist Hospital in Memphis. Hodge eventually got his precious cargo to the proper facility, and Priscilla gave birth to Lisa Marie at 5:01 P.M.

* * *

Had Lisa Marie been born a boy, she would have been named John Baron by Elvis and Priscilla. Marie was the name of Colonel Parker's wife.

* * *

Lisa Marie was spoiled by her superrich and famous father. She cruised around Graceland in the customized chrome golf cart that he bought for her.

When she was nine years old, Elvis gave her a custom-made full-length mink coat and a smiley-face ring that was fitted with diamonds for eyes. But Priscilla didn't want her little girl spoiled by Daddy's big bucks. So Mommy told a little white lie and said the fur and the ring were fake.

On another occasion, Priscilla got peeved at her husband because he slipped five dollars beneath his daughter's pillow after she'd lost a tooth. Mom was mad because while playing Tooth Fairy a previous time, she'd placed only fifty cents under Lisa Marie's pillow.

"The key to being a good parent is making the children behave whether they want to or not."

A Kind and Benevolent King

Heart of Gold

Whether it was King-size cars or stacks of cash, Elvis was quick to dish out generous gifts to friends, family, and even complete strangers. His mind-boggling benevolence has never been fully recorded, but it's clear he spread his wealth like no other performer.

Elvis once said, "Sharin' money is what gives it value." And the big-hearted singer certainly shared his money—especially among people he didn't even know.

"Whenever he saw someone in need, he wanted to help," recalled his stepbrother David Stanley. "Whenever he would read in the newspaper about a family being burned out or evicted, he would have one of us call the editor to find out how he could help. He gave away thousands of dollars in that way."

Stanley said Elvis once met a family in severe financial trouble because the bread-winner had lost his job. Presley wound up paying off their debts, and buying them a new house and three new Cadillacs.

When Elvis read in the newspaper that an elderly woman needed a new wheelchair, he went out and bought her an electric one and personally delivered it to her along with two hundred dollars in cash.

After learning that an Arkansas police officer lost a leg in a car crash in the line of duty, Elvis was there to help. Officer James Bullock was recovering at his home in Marion when he received a check for one thousand dollars from Presley, who had heard about the injury on the radio.

Elvis sometimes would give expensive gifts for no apparent reason.

One lucky lady was presented with a new Eldorado, along with enough money for a new wardrobe and a vacation with her husband, after a chance encounter with Elvis in Memphis.

When Elvis was in the hospital once, he gave new automobiles to a trio of his nurses.

Then there was the time Presley saw a woman looking at his custom Cadillac while he browsed for a new one at a Memphis dealership in 1974. The singer informed the woman that the car she was ogling wasn't for sale. Then he floored the woman by telling her to go inside and select the new Caddy of her choice!

* * *

Members of his entourage, the Memphis Mafia, didn't make that much money—about $425 a week in the 1970s—but Elvis often gave them big bonuses, bought them cars, and even paid their down payments on houses.

One year he bought nineteen Cadillacs for the members of his staff!

* * *

The King had a supersoft heart when it came to charitable organizations. During the peak of his moneymaking days, Elvis would donate as much as $100,000 a year to a variety of good causes. Benefiting most from Elvis's fat wallet were the March of Dimes, YMCA, YWCA, Muscular Dystrophy Association, Cerebral Palsy Association, Boys Town, Father Tom's Indian School, Salvation Army, and the Motion Picture Relief Fund.

Presley didn't limit himself to cash donations. He once handed over the keys to a $35,000 Rolls Royce and requested it be auctioned off with the proceeds going to charity. SHARE—a Hollywood women's nonprofit organization for mentally retarded children—was the grateful charity that benefited from this act of kindness in 1968.

Another time, the King made waves by donating the former presidential yacht of Franklin Delano Roosevelt, the *Potomac,* which he had once owned. He gave it to St. Jude's Children's Hospital, which sold it for $55,000.

In 1965, Elvis donated $50,000 to the Motion Picture Relief Fund in Hollywood, a sum which at the time was the largest single donation the charity had ever received.

* * *

Although he's mainly linked to Memphis, Elvis was born in East Tupelo, Mississippi, and he never forgot his roots there. He helped his hometown construct a youth center, then established a scholarship fund for needy students.

* * *

After the deadly Hurricane Camille ravaged the Gulf Coast in 1975, Elvis gave a concert in Jackson, Mississippi, for the benefit of the victims. The concert raised over $100,000.

Gift-Giver to the Stars

It wasn't only the truly needy who were on the receiving end of an Elvis gift. Heavyweight boxing champion Muhammad Ali was every bit as popular as Elvis when he accepted a gaudy $10,000 robe from the King.

Elvis explained, "No one ever gives the rich presents." He was most pleased when Ali wore the robe into the ring for his 1973 title bout against underdog Ken Norton. The crowd got a good look at the back of the snazzy robe, where Elvis had ordered a seamstress to attach the title "The People's Champion."

Unfortunately for both Ali and Elvis, the champ suffered one of his few ring losses that day—and later blamed it on the gift robe!

Superstitious Ali suffered a broken jaw and later mumbled that the glitzy garment must have been cursed. The fighter had the jinxed robe stored away and never wore it again.

* * *

Elvis formed a mutual admiration society with singer-dancer Sammy Davis Jr. and managed to catch his act three times. Presley was so impressed by "The Candy Man" that he once pulled a $30,000, 157-karat black sapphire ring from his own finger and handed it to the speechless Davis as a gift.

In a way, Elvis owed Sammy, who had first crack at recording the touching tune "In the Ghetto." Producers offered the song to Davis, but later turned it over to Elvis because they didn't like the way his pal approached the serious message of the song. Elvis offered them a much more acceptable "feeling" for the lyrics, and it became a huge hit for him.

* * *

In 1975, country singer T.G. Sheppard was given a customized GMC bus by his friend Elvis. Of course, the gift may have had something to do with T.G.'s introduction of Linda Thompson to Elvis. The former beauty queen became Presley's main squeeze for the next two years.

* * *

Marvin Robertson Jr. was a member of the singing group the Young Americans when he met up with Elvis on a United Airlines flight in 1969. The two singers were casually conversing on a long trip from Honolulu to Los Angeles when Robertson told Elvis how much he liked the sparkling ring the King was sporting. Elvis watched Robertson's jaw drop as he immediately removed the $2,500 piece of jewelry and handed it over to him.

* * *

Among the more offbeat gifts from Elvis were a new kidney for his music producer and a more streamlined nose for a disc jockey friend.

RCA music producer Felton Jarvis helped give Elvis's singing career new life in the 1970s by getting him to record the right kind of music. Elvis was appreciative and returned the favor by financing a transplant operation for the ailing Felton, who was desperately in need of a new kidney.

Memphis disc jockey George Klein "nose" he benefited from his friendship with high school classmate Elvis. When Klein went on to spin records for WKEM, he slipped in an on-air live performance of "Keep Them Icy Fingers Off Me" by Elvis early in the singer's career.

The favor was never forgotten by Elvis, who gladly plunked down the money when Klein needed plastic surgery on his nose years later.

* * *

Gil Gilliland, Presley's personal hairstylist for many years, received Elvis's famed $10,000 gold lamé suit as a gift.

Giving Away a King's Ransom

Elvis often showered his fans with surprise—and expensive gifts.

During a 1975 concert, Elvis was crooning his popular hit "Can't Help Falling in Love" when he spotted in the audience a five-year-old girl who reminded him of his precious daughter, Lisa Marie, who was seven at the time.

Elvis slowly made his way to the child, whose name was Rhonda Boler, sang a verse in front of the girl and her stunned mother, and then handed the Lisa Marie look-alike his expensive diamond medallion cross!

While performing in Asheville, North Carolina, in 1975, Elvis doled out much more than his greatest hits. He also handed out pieces of his own jewelry valued at a combined $220,000 to about a dozen shocked but happy fans.

Driven to Kindness

Elvis was driven by an obsession to give away expensive automobiles. He fitted a small army of men and women with flashy cars and thought nothing of walking into dealerships and buying an entire line of one type of vehicle—usually Cadillacs or Lincolns—to give away as gifts.

In 1975 alone, he purchased over fifty new cars for friends and strangers. One day that year, Presley bought the entire fleet of Cadillac Eldorados on the lot of Madison Cadillac in Memphis to give away as gifts.

The year before, Elvis walked into the Schilling Lincoln-Mercury dealership in Memphis and purchased the dealership's entire stock of Lincoln Continental Mark IVs. The five cars came in aqua, black, blue, red, and silver and set the singer back over $60,000.

Elvis made a similar mass purchase at the Kumpf Lincoln-Mercury car dealership in Denver. The deep-pocketed vacationer dropped $70,000 on January 14, 1976, while buying five cars as gifts for friends he met in Vail, Colorado. Elvis was marking his forty-first birthday at the ski resort when he decided to reverse the normal routine for a birthday. Rather than receive gifts, he handed out the shiny four-wheeled packages to his friends.

Both Denver police captain Jerry Kennedy and his wife were handed the keys to his and hers Elvis-bought Lincoln Continental Mark IVs. Captain Kennedy once worked as a security guard for the singer. Two other police officials were also given Mark IVs.

After reporting about the Presley gifts, Colorado newscaster Don Kinney joked on the air, "I'd rather have a little sports car." The next day, a Seville was delivered to the stunned newscaster, compliments of Elvis.

* * *

Among the many recipients of cars from Elvis were:

* His maid Alberta, who in 1956 got an auto so she wouldn't have to take the bus to work when the Presley family moved to the Graceland estate.

* Dr. Sydney Boyers, who treated Elvis after the performer became ill during a Las Vegas show in 1973. In addition to receiving his normal fee, the doctor was given a new white Lincoln Continental.

* Karate champion Dave Hebler, who worked as a personal bodyguard in 1974. The appreciative performer got a kick out of handing Hebler the keys to a Mercedes.

* Graceland cook Mary Jenkins, who whipped up Presley's favorite foods from 1963 until his death in 1977. The kitchen wiz was well paid for her culinary kindness—Elvis bought her a new Cadillac, six other vehicles, and a new house!

* High school buddy and Memphis Mafia member Marty Lacker. The man who served with Joe Esposito as co-best man at the wedding of Elvis and Priscilla in 1967 was later presented a Cadillac.

* Cook and maid Pauline Nicholson who worked fifteen years at Graceland. Elvis bought her a brand-new 1964 Buick LeSabre.

* Korean-born Kang Rhee, the man who taught Elvis martial arts at the Institute of Self-Defense in Memphis. Kang became a good friend of Elvis, and the singer showed his appreciation by giving Kang a custom 1973 Eldorado Cadillac and $50,000 to build a new karate school.

* Cook and maid Nancy Rooks. She was cruising in her first-ever new car, a yellow 1974 Pontiac Ventura, thanks to her gracious Graceland employer.

* Memphis Mafia member Jerry Schilling. He was such a good friend that he received several new cars and had his wedding tab picked up by Elvis.

* Wardrobe man Al Strada. The clothing coordinator owned a new Porsche thanks to his well-dressed employer.

* Bodyguard and buddy Sonny West and his brother Red West. Over the years, Elvis gave Sonny a black Cadillac convertible, a motorcycle, a pickup truck, and several other vehicles. Brother Red had no reason to be green with envy. He acquired a collection that included a new Mercedes-Benz, a new Cadillac Eldorado convertible, a pickup truck, and a motorcycle.

* * *

When Elvis proposed to Ginger Alden in 1977, he gave her a $50,000, eleven-and-a-half-karat engagement ring. "Elvis was so delighted when I accepted his proposal," Alden told reporters, "that he telephoned a local auto dealer and had a navy blue Mark V given to the jeweler as a thank-you present." The jeweler was Lowell Hays, who over the years had sold Elvis over $800,000 worth of jewelry.

* * *

One day Presley's personal assistant, Alan Fortas, was taking his bride to meet Elvis when they got into an accident that totaled their car but left them uninjured. Recalled Fortas, "When I got to Graceland and told Elvis what had happened, he said, 'You have a dollar?' I handed it over—and he gave me his wife Priscilla's year-old Corvair."

"Money is meant to be spread around.
The more happiness it helps to create, the more it's worth.
It's worthless as old cut-up paper if it just lays
in a bank and grows there without ever
having been used to help a body."

Lights! Camera! Action!

Movie Madness

Here are little-known facts about some of Elvis's films:

LOVE ME TENDER

Presley's first words on the silver screen, as Clint Reno, were: "Whoa! . . . Brett, Vance. They told us you were dead!" His dying words were: "Everything's gonna be all right."

* * *

Actor Neville Brand, the man who "killed" Elvis in the movie, was the fourth most-decorated American soldier in World War II.

* * *

An ending was filmed in which Elvis lived, but it was decided not to use it. When Presley's character died, so many fans were outraged—including Elvis's mother—that Colonel Parker agreed never to have Elvis play a death scene again.

* * *

For his performance, Elvis was given a "Worst Supporting Actor Award" by the Harvard *Lampoon*.

* * *

Love Me Tender was the only film in which Elvis did not receive top billing. Richard Egan and Debra Paget were billed ahead of the singer.

* * *

There's a blooper in the film, which is supposed to be set at the close of the Civil War. As Paget cries by her window, you can catch a glimpse of a car off in the distance.

JAILHOUSE ROCK

Elvis capped off a dance number from his 1957 film *Jailhouse Rock* by accidentally inhaling one of his porcelain caps. The dental disaster led to awful chest pains when the cap became lodged inside one of the star's lungs.

Presley was rushed to Cedars of Lebanon Hospital in Los Angeles, where doctors yanked the faux tooth from the patient's chest cavity.

* * *

MGM's commissary added to its menu crisp bacon, mashed potatoes, and brown gravy during the filming because they were among Elvis's favorite foods.

* * *

Elvis refused to shave his sideburns for his role in the film, so they were "erased" by a talented makeup artist.

* * *

On the last day of filming, Elvis became a hero. A small heater in the dressing room of costar Jennifer Holden caught fire. While studio hands put out the fire, Elvis carried Jennifer to safety.

FLAMING STAR

Elvis wore brown contact lenses in a screen test because his character was part white and part Indian. But producers scrapped the idea of the lenses.

* * *

A stuntman was hired to double for Elvis in the tough fight scenes, but he wasn't needed because Presley proved he could handle himself in the brawls.

During one staged fight, Elvis broke the arm of close friend Red West, who was portraying an Indian.

* * *

Elvis attempted his first serious acting role in which he did not sing. The movie bombed. From then on, every Presley movie included scenes of him singing.

* * *

The movie was banned in South Africa because the strict racial laws prohibited showing a film featuring a mixed-race character.

WILD IN THE COUNTRY

Talk about a hard-headed star! In a scene opposite one of his costars, Millie Perkins, Elvis took a slap to the face—and Perkins cried out in pain. She had broken her wrist from striking him.

* * *

During the production, Elvis was treated for boils on his bottom.

* * *

Readers of *Teen* magazine voted Elvis and costar Tuesday Weld the "Damp Raincoat Award" for Most Disappointing Performers of 1961.

IT HAPPENED AT THE WORLD'S FAIR

MGM arranged for a hundred special policemen to protect Elvis from World's Fair crowds while filming on location. Six Pinkerton plainclothes detectives were at his side every second he wasn't in front of the camera.

* * *

Elvis's wardrobe included ten suits, four sport coats, thirty shirts, fifteen pairs of pants, two cashmere coats, and fifty-five ties.

CLAMBAKE

Production was halted for several days when Elvis whisked off to Las Vegas to tie the knot with Priscilla. The honeymoon, however, was cut short so Elvis could finish the film.

* * *

A pudgy Presley showed up on the set weighing more than two hundred pounds. The weight problem didn't suit director Arthur Nadel, who ordered a strict diet and plenty of wardrobe alterations. The star's unsightly rolls were kept under wraps with the help of several concealing jackets.

* * *

95

Principal shooting was delayed for two weeks after Elvis slipped in his bathroom, hit his head, and suffered a concussion.

* * *

The white suit worn by Elvis in the movie was supposedly worth $10,000. It was later cut into small pieces with snippets going into his four-record boxed set of *Elvis: The Other Sides—Worldwide Gold Award Hits, Vol. 2.*

* * *

The movie is supposed to take place in Florida, yet in several scenes, mountains can be seen in the background. Since Florida is remarkably flat, it's a sure sign those exteriors were not filmed in the Sunshine State.

★ LIVE A LITTLE, LOVE A LITTLE

While filming in downtown Los Angeles, Elvis was knocked to the pavement by a pair of elderly fans. But they weren't after the rock 'n' roller. The excited oldsters pushed the stunned singer out of the way so they could get the autograph of his costar—legendary crooner Rudy Vallee.

* * *

Vernon Presley played an extra sitting at a table.

* * *

The Hollywood Women's Press Club named Elvis recipient of their 1967 Least Cooperative Actor of the Year award. Joining Elvis was Least Cooperative Actress Natalie Wood.

Music Madness

For "Hound Dog," his first record released under the RCA label, Elvis did thirty-one takes of the song in the recording session. The one finally chosen was the eighteenth take. Presley would have done as many takes as the producer wanted, said D.J. Fontana, Elvis's first drummer.

"He had a keen ear," said Fontana. "He wasn't a fantastic musician, but he played just enough to know what he was talking about. And when he heard what he wanted to hear, he'd say, 'That's it, man, don't change nothin'.'"

* * *

"Elvis warmed up on gospel music," said guitarist Chip Young. "That's how he opened up his throat. He did 'Amazing Grace' every time."

* * *

To get the echoing sound for the smash hit "Heartbreak Hotel," Elvis recorded the tune in a stairwell at the RCA studios in Nashville.

* * *

Despite his eighteen No. 1 records and a monstrous library of memorable songs, Elvis earned a mere three Grammy Awards in his lifetime.

And these crowning achievements for the King of Rock 'n' Roll came in the field of religious recordings! Elvis, who in his career received fourteen Grammy nominations, was given the Lifetime Achievement Award in 1971 at the age of thirty-six.

* * *

In 1984, RCA records announced Elvis was officially responsible for the sale of a mind-boggling one billion records. To better understand this figure, just consider that every American man, woman, and child could claim four Elvis records. Laid end to end, the monumental collection would wrap around the earth more than twice.

* * *

From the day his first record was pressed until his death in 1977, Elvis's career earnings were estimated at a whopping $4.3 billion.

The take comes from 650 LPs, EPs, and singles; thirty-one movies; countless concert and TV appearances; and merchandising.

* * *

Presley boasted 107 Top 40 hits (compared to forty-nine for the Beatles) and another forty-two that made the charts. Seventeen Presley singles went gold. Of his ninety albums, thirty-two went gold (500,000 sales), eight went platinum (one million sold), and two went multiplatinum (two million).

Despite his death, Elvis CDs, tapes, merchandising, licensing, and income from Graceland continue to soar.

* * *

The word "Blue" or "Blues" appears in the title of eighteen songs recorded by Elvis. The individual titles include: "Beach Boy Blues," "Blueberry Hill," "Blue Christmas," "Blue Eyes Crying in the Rain," "Blue Hawaii," "Blue Moon," "Blue Moon of Kentucky," "Blue River," "Blue Suede Shoes," "G.I. Blues," "Indescribably Blue," "Mean Woman Blues," "A Mess of Blues," "Milkcow Blues Boogie," "Moody Blue," "Something Blue," "Steamroller Blues," and "When My Blue Moon Turns to Gold Again."

Live . . . and in Person . . .

Presley's 1973 "Aloha From Hawaii" special was seen by an estimated worldwide audience of 1.5 billion people. The figures were truly out of this world, since more Americans watched the King singing than saw astronaut Neil Armstrong walking on the moon!

* * *

Elvis picked up some of his onstage dance moves from watching old movies featuring Polish dancer Marianna Michalska (1901–1959). Colonel Parker suggested his budding star watch the dancer do her thing in movies like *The Devil Dancer, Piccadilly,* and *Aloma of the South Seas.* Elvis did just that and came away with some nifty new moves from the woman credited with inventing the "shimmy."

* * *

In 1969 when Elvis returned to live performing after an eight-year absence from the concert scene, he would change from one gaudy jumpsuit to another during each concert.

On opening night at the International Hotel in Las Vegas, Presley, who was dressed in a white jumpsuit, felt very nervous. "If the songs don't go over, we can always do a medley of costumes," he told his friends. But his songs did go over—and so did his costume changes.

In fact, he got so used to switching clothes that during recording sessions he often changed his clothes three times a day, as if he were still in concert.

* * *

Each of the custom jumpsuits worn in concert by Elvis had a name. They were known as: Peacock, American Eagle, Indian, Sundial, Burning Love, Red Lion, Nail Studded Suit, White Prehistoric Bird, Flame, Blue Prehistoric Bird, White Eagle, Tiffany, Black Eagle, Blue Aztec, Red Eagle, Blue Rainbow, Sleek, Inca Gold Leaf, Gypsy, Mexican Sundial, Blue Braid, Blue Swirl, Flower, Blue Rainbow, Mad Tiger, and King of Spades.

* * *

During one concert in Lincoln, Nebraska, screaming fans streamed down to the edge of the stage, hoping to get near Elvis. A no-nonsense police officer, standing below where Presley was singing, lost his head, grabbed a young boy, and flung him like a rag doll into the surging crowd.

Elvis saw this blatant act of brutality and decided to make the officer pay for his transgression. Elvis tossed one of his scarves at the officer, knowing full well that the fans would converge on him in a desperate attempt to get the prized Presley memento. Then Elvis tossed another scarf, and then another. And each time, the fans knocked down the officer in the mad scramble. Finally, the officer limped off toward the nearest exit.

Presley Fan-demonium

Elvis wound up with a huge collection of teddy bears because of rumors that he liked them.

During his January 6, 1957, appearance on "The Ed Sullivan Show," Elvis revealed his fans sent him 282 teddy bears for Christmas. After hearing that, fans sent him thousands more. Presley donated the teddy bears to charity.

* * *

In 1956, four determined girls captured Elvis and held him hostage in his hotel in New Orleans. The wild bunch bound and gagged an elevator operator, then held Elvis between floors for an hour. It may have been the first time the King performed before a truly captive audience.

* * *

It wasn't unusual for female fans to enclose their photograph when writing a letter to their idol. Elvis of course didn't have the time to read every letter he received from these lovestruck ladies. However, he did have his secretaries pull photographs of the prettiest girls and place them in albums.

The curious King would drop by just to leaf through this amazing gallery of girls. The gracious star shared the wealth of women with his buddies and sometimes they'd pursue one of the beauties.

The more brazen fans would sometimes stoop to sending sexually explicit snapshots. These perverse photos were dumped into a desk drawer later tabbed "the dirty file." Friends say Elvis found little satisfaction from inspecting the porno posers. The dirty file apparently had much more appeal to his pals.

"Only thing worse than watchin'
a bad movie is bein' in one."

Elvis and the Colonel

The Colonel Leads the Charge

He was known as Col. Tom Parker from West Virginia. But Presley's notorious iron-fisted, money-grubbing manager was really a Dutch national who lied about his birth. In fact, he never became an American citizen, nor was he ever a real colonel.

Parker was born Andreas Cornelius van Kujik in Holland. The Dutchman claimed Huntington, West Virginia, as his place of birth. Although he never applied for citizenship in the United States, Parker swore allegiance to our country when he joined the army in 1929.

Parker got his start in show business by mingling with the sideshow performers and midway freaks of the American Royal show, a big-time carnival that toured throughout the South. He learned the ins and outs of marketing during his ten-year stint.

When he went out on his own, he formed the Greater Parker Pony Circus, where he proved to be a smooth hustler. He painted sparrows yellow and sold them as canaries. He sold "foot-long" hot dogs that were nothing more than foot-long buns with a bit of hot dog sticking out of each end and the middle filled with chopped onions.

One of the acts that he featured was his "dancing chickens." The birds would hop around to the tune of a record. What the public didn't know was that the chickens weren't dancing. They were hopping around because they were standing on a hot plate covered with sawdust.

During the winter months, Parker was a dog catcher in Tampa, Florida. He eventually became a carny press agent and worked his way into the country and western music scene. Before long, he began managing such stars as Hank Snow and Eddy Arnold.

But Parker was fired by Arnold. In the summer of 1955 Parker saw the enormous potential of a raw rock 'n' roller named Elvis Presley, so he went after the young talent. The Colonel began meeting the talented teen and his parents at various concerts. Parker visited them at their home in Memphis, promising them millions of dollars if he could manage Elvis.

Vernon encouraged Elvis to sign on with Parker. But Gladys distrusted the Colonel. So Parker asked Hank Snow, who was his business partner, to help sway Gladys. Snow convinced her that Elvis would be in good hands because Snow would look out for her son. So Gladys agreed. But Parker then signed the naive young singer to a lifetime contract that gave the Colonel total control over Elvis's career—and eventually squeezed Snow completely out of the picture.

It wouldn't be long before Elvis blasted off with Colonel Parker at the controls. As the singer's manager, Parker worked his way up to a whopping 50 percent commission, eventually earning more than his bankable client. The shrewd manager took half of what Elvis earned from 1967 on—plus an extra salary as a technical adviser on Presley's films.

* * *

Parker was not a real colonel.

Louisiana governor Jimmy Davis bestowed Tom Parker with his honorary title of colonel in 1948. The ceremonial ranking was the brainchild of a Davis staffer who used to work with Parker during his carnival days.

Parker began insisting everyone call him Colonel. Five years later, he was also made an honorary Colonel by the governor of Tennessee. That title was bestowed in exchange for Parker's assistance during a political campaign.

What Might Have Been

Elvis missed out on several fantastic and memorable opportunities to perform because of Colonel Parker's greed and deceit.

Presley would have performed at the White House for President Richard Nixon, but Colonel Parker squashed the deal by insisting on $25,000 for the show. White House protocol doesn't include payments for performers.

Elvis never performed on Dick Clark's "American Bandstand" because Clark paid the artists on his show union scale. Colonel Parker demanded thousands of dollars more for Presley to appear.

Life magazine wanted to make Elvis its cover boy in 1960 upon his triumphant return from the army. But once again, Colonel Parker pulled the rug out from under his client by demanding $25,000 from the magazine for the privilege of printing the cover shot. The picture and a planned feature story on Elvis were scrapped.

Presley had the chance to perform with Arthur Fiedler and the Boston Pops, but Parker turned it down because it wasn't for enough money.

In 1961, Elvis was invited to put on a show before Queen Elizabeth II in London at the Royal Command Variety Performance. It was an incredible honor—especially for a rock 'n' roller. Only the world's top entertainers were ever invited to the renowned annual event.

But Colonel Parker refused to let Elvis go. The reason had nothing to do with the star, but everything to do with the manager.

Other than when Presley was in the army, Parker seldom let Elvis perform anywhere without being by his side. If Presley were to go to England, Parker needed to be there with him. But Parker was afraid to leave the country because he wasn't an American citizen. If he applied for an American passport, his alien status would have been discovered and he feared he would be deported.

Because the Colonel wouldn't allow Elvis to go on his own, Presley missed out on numerous opportunities to perform in Europe, Australia, and Japan. The singer's fans in other countries were left yearning for the chance to see the star perform live.

Greed Is Good

Although Parker helped make Elvis millions of dollars, the Colonel never gave Presley the chance to develop a serious acting career.

That's because the manager was only interested in making money. "I consider it my solemn duty to put Elvis in the 90 percent tax bracket," he claimed. When it came to movies, the basic consideration for whether he would let Elvis sign for the role was money. Parker once said, "Anybody who will pay my boy a million dollars can make any kind of picture he wants."

As a result, Presley starred in movies that made grade-B flicks look like Oscar winners. Parker cared so little about the quality of Presley's films he once admitted that he didn't always read the scripts—only the amount on the checks from the producers.

Parker's money-grubbing reputation knew no bounds in Hollywood. While doing a scene for the movie *Blue Hawaii,* Elvis ran out of the surf and straight into the camera. But Parker suddenly jumped into the shot and waved his arms to stop the shooting. Ignoring the furious director, Parker turned to producer Hal Wallis and pointed to Presley's wristwatch.

"Do you remember the terms of Elvis's contract?" Parker asked. "It says that Elvis doesn't provide his own clothes. If you want his watch in the picture, you'll have to pay us twenty-five grand." The disgusted Wallis shook his head and asked Presley to take off his watch, which the singer did.

Elvis in *West Side Story?*

Because of Colonel Parker's outrageous demands for money, Presley missed out on several top movie roles.

Elvis had first crack to play Tony in *West Side Story,* the Kris Kristofferson role in *A Star Is Born*, the Paul Newman part in *Sweet Bird of Youth,* the Tony Curtis role in *The Defiant Ones*, the Robert Mitchum part in *Thunder Road*, and Jon Voigt's street hustler role in *Midnight Cowboy.*

But Colonel Parker nixed all those parts because the proposed salary for his client wasn't big enough. The manager was content to stick with his strategy of "quantity over quality" in Presley's movie career.

* * *

Screen sex goddess Jayne Mansfield wanted Elvis to play a part in her 1956 film *The Girl Can't Help It,* but profit-minded Parker again cost his client the role. The Colonel insisted on $50,000 for Elvis to croon just one song for the picture.

Mansfield was miffed, but she tried to soften the star's demand by spending several days in seclusion with Elvis. The tactic didn't work because it was Colonel Parker who needed the softening.

* * *

In the early 1970s, Elvis asked his father, Vernon, to fire Parker. When Vernon tried to can the Colonel, Parker pulled out an itemized bill for five million dollars and said that's what Elvis owed him if he were fired. Vernon backed off, and Elvis chose not to take on Parker himself.

What's Next? Elvis Toilet Paper?

The Colonel looked at Presley's film career as a major marketing tool.

Presley was merchandised like few celebrities before him. There were Elvis necklaces, photographs, mittens, bracelets, shoes, stuffed hound dogs, pen pal magazines, toreador pants, Bermuda shorts, ball-point pens, dolls, buttons, colognes, soda pop, bubble gum cards, board games, pajamas, belts, and glow-in-the-dark autographed pictures. There was little regard for taste or quality.

During the 1950s, girls longing to get their lips on Elvis could settle for the next best thing—Elvis lipstick. The product came in six tempting shades: Tender Pink, Heartbreak Pink, Love-Ya Fuchsia, Hound Dog Orange, Tutti Frutti Red, and Cruel Red.

Confectioners whipped up a Love Me Tender candy bar in 1956. Unwrapped ones aren't so tender anymore but they can fetch a sweet price from collectors.

Elvis's army induction gave Parker the chance to add another novelty item to sell to adoring Elvis fans. He sold them imitation dog tags stamped with Elvis's name, rank, and serial number—which was US53310761.

* * *

Parker helped set up Elvis fan clubs all over the world. Any kind of demographic group would work—teens, grandmas, soldiers.

He called upon his kooky carnival days to come up with the Elvis Presley Midget Fan Club. He gathered a few dozen little people at a Chicago hotel. Then he arranged for them to meet in Memphis, where they marched through town, advertising both the fan club and an upcoming concert.

* * *

Colonel Parker began writing an autobiography in 1956. He titled the book *The Benevolent Con Man (How Much Does It Cost If It's Free?)*. One publisher offered him a $100,000 advance—a huge amount at the time.

But the Colonel sniffed: "Well, I guess I could let you have the back cover for that!" The publisher declined. Parker planned to run full-page ads between chapters. He figured advertisers would gladly shell out $25,000 for such prime locations. But the Colonel never wrote the book.

The Hypnotic Parker

Colonel Parker sometimes hypnotized members of Presley's Memphis Mafia—and had them on all fours barking like dogs.

Singer-composer-producer Phil Spector once raised the specter of concern that Elvis was being hypnotized by Parker. Spector, the only man to produce for both Elvis and the Beatles, voiced his accusations after discovering Parker practiced hypnosis, often on Presley's close friends.

Colonel Parker boasted about his hypnotic abilities. In fact, he said it worked on animals too. He claimed he used hypnosis to round up strays while he served as a Tampa dogcatcher in the 1940s.

Parker later used his powers to make members of Presley's entourage behave like mutts.

Presley's bodyguard and friend Sonny West told reporters how Parker would hypnotize members of the Memphis Mafia. "He [Parker] would make us get down on all fours and tell us that we were dogs," West recalled. "He would have us barking and yelping like dogs and snapping at each other."

John O'Grady, a private detective who worked for Elvis, got angry after witnessing one of these shameful displays. Recalled O'Grady, "I remember once in one of the dressing rooms, Parker told Charlie Hodge to get down on all fours and bark like a dog—and poor, dumb Charlie did it. I looked at Parker and told him, 'If you ever said something like that to me, I'd push your damned head through the wall.'"

The King Is Dead! Long Live the Profits!

The ever-calculating Colonel wasted little time grieving after learning Elvis had died. Immediately after getting the sad news, the money-grubbing manager launched into a frenzied day of phone calls to ensure he could merchandise the dead superstar.

The very next day after Presley's death, Parker had procured a $150,000 advance on the sale of Elvis souvenir rights and worked a deal that would net him a hefty 78 percent of the proceeds. The profit-minded Parker may have lost a client, but he gained a fortune from the post-death dealings.

If he felt saddened by Presley's death, Parker didn't show it. At Elvis's funeral, the Colonel declined to be one of the pallbearers. He shocked and dismayed Presley's family, friends, and fans by wearing shorts, a colorful shirt, and a baseball cap at the funeral services while all the others in attendance were appropriately dressed.

* * *

Parker continued to work feverishly on making money off of Elvis after the singer's death. The Colonel came up with the marketing slogan "Always Elvis." Among the merchandising deals he inked was one with an Italian winery to market an "Always Elvis" brand in the United States. It didn't matter that Elvis was never known as a wine drinker.

A short year after the singer's untimely demise, Colonel Parker held the first Always Elvis Convention in Las Vegas. On hand to push products linked to the dead superstar were Vernon, Priscilla, and Lisa Marie Presley.

Fans paid fifteen dollars each to gaze upon a mountain of Elvis memorabilia that included the dead singer's stage costumes.

But the highlight of the festival was the unveiling of a life-size bronze statue of Elvis. Vernon, Priscilla, and Lisa Marie pulled on gold ropes that lifted the plush red velvet curtain which was covering the statue. The crowd naturally pressed forward to capture photos of the impressive statue, but security stepped in to quiet the cameras. After all, photos of the bronze Elvis could be purchased at the souvenir counter for a mere two dollars.

* * *

The gravy train screeched to a halt for Colonel Parker when Vernon Presley passed away on June 26, 1979—the day of the Colonel's seventieth birthday. A probate judge scoured through the many money-making deals involving Colonel Parker and the Elvis estate. When the dust settled, the manager was forced to sever all connections with the estate. The Presley family finally regained control of the Elvis money-making machine, and Parker went into a comfortable retirement.

"People say the Colonel has a good thing in me.
Sure he has. And I've got a good thing in him."

The Spiritual Elvis

Elvis the Healer

Elvis believed God had blessed him with the power to heal others.

On several occasions, Presley showed he could ease the pain of friends by laying his hands on them. His aide, Dean Nichopoulos, son of the King's personal physician, Dr. George Nichopoulos, felt his boss's healing powers during a ski trip in Colorado. Dean was screaming with pain after falling and twisting his leg in a skiing accident. When Elvis reached his side, the singer bent down and put both his hands on Dean's aching leg. The rest of Presley's entourage watched with bemusement and discussed the best way to get the injured man to a hospital.

Then suddenly, Dean stopped crying out in anguish. He sat up with a relieved look on his face and declared, "Hey! It doesn't hurt anymore!" Then he leaped to his feet and walked back to the lodge.

Presley's stepbrother David Stanley often talked about the amazing healing powers of Elvis. David said that several times the singer cured him of blinding headaches simply by laying his hands on Stanley's throbbing head. "Sure enough, in a matter of minutes, the headache would be completely gone," recalled Stanley.

* * *

Presley believed his first name was religiously significant.

Elvis discovered "El" was a common contraction of the name Elohim, the God of the ancient Hebrews, and "Vis" was an Orientally derived word for force or power. Therefore, he thought, Elvis had the power of God working on his side. Such belief only served to bolster his conviction that he possessed divine powers.

On one occasion he stunned several of his pals when he raised his hand through the sunroof of the car in which they were traveling and parted a nasty thunderstorm.

The King and his pals were driving from Las Vegas to Palm Springs when they noticed the violent storm dead ahead.

"Boy, we're really in for it," noted one of the guys.

Elvis, who was driving, calmly responded, "I'll take care of it." As the car entered the storm, Elvis thrust his hand up through the open sunroof and shouted, "I order you to let us pass through! I order you to move to the side and leave us alone!"

The passengers later swore that the dark clouds parted for them. The car raced down the road with heavy rain to their left and right, but none striking their car.

Elvis and the Bible

Elvis was deeply religious and carried the Bible with him wherever he went. He also carried a picture of Jesus in his wallet. As an avid reader of the Bible, Presley once boasted that he had copies of the Good Book in every room of his houses in both Memphis and California.

During one concert, the King brought the crowd to a dead silence when a fan approached the stage and handed him a Bible. Elvis flipped through the familiar book, stopping now and then to read some of its passages out loud to his audience.

According to David Stanley, Elvis always longed to be a minister. He sometimes held Bible studies at home for young, beautiful female fans—women who had other things on their minds than learning scripture. "Looking back on it now, it's funny that we [Elvis and his pals] would spend so much time talking about Christianity because we weren't living a very spiritual life," said Stanley.

"Every so often, Elvis would decide he needed purification, so he would abstain from sex or medication . . . and he expected the same from us."

* * *

Elvis wore both a cross and a Star of David. When asked about the double display of religious symbols, he responded: "I don't want to miss out on heaven because of a technicality."

* * *

Elvis and the Occult

Even though he was raised a Baptist, Presley was often immersed in a book about the occult, numerology, or some other psychic phenomenon.

In 1964, his hairstylist, Larry Geller, introduced Elvis to the world of the occult. Over the years, the men grew close and began to discuss such mystical topics as parapsychology, religion, the supernatural, and life after death.

Elvis was intrigued with death since first learning his twin brother Jesse Garon had been stillborn. As a young boy, Elvis would sneak into a Memphis funeral home at night and look at the bodies laid out for burial. Later, the devastating loss of his beloved mother, Gladys, only served to encourage the King to dig deeper into the meaning of life.

Geller became a guru to Elvis. It got to the point where Elvis wouldn't leave home without two trunks filled with books on the occult and paranormal. The Graceland library held 250 such books, most of which were suggested by his trusted pal Geller. The relationship bothered Colonel Parker, who didn't like Geller's growing control over his number one client. Parker insisted a third party be present at all times when Geller cut Presley's hair. Parker eventually broke Geller's hold on Elvis and then had the book-filled trunks and their contents burned.

"Religion is like music. You experience them and they both move you."

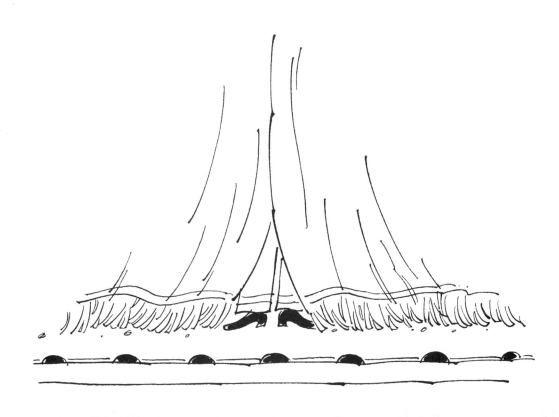

The Final Curtain

The King Is Dead

Elvis sensed his own death was near just three days before he died.

David Stanley claimed that Elvis knew he was going to die.

On August 13, 1977, Stanley sat with Elvis in his bedroom, watching television and talking. "I was struck by how tired he looked—tired and strangely sad," recalled Stanley, who wrote the book *Life with Elvis*. "I would have taken him for someone who had worked all his life in a factory or a coal mine—not for the King of Rock 'n' Roll.

"I was about to take a trip out of town, so I told Elvis, 'I'll see you in a couple of days.' Elvis shook his head. 'No, David. No you won't see me in a couple of days. The next time I see you, it will be in another time, another place. David, you won't ever see me again . . . alive.'

"'Hey man, don't talk that way!' I said.

"He shook my hand. 'I'll save a place for you. You can be sure of that.'"

Stanley said he tried to joke with Elvis, but Presley gave him a bear hug and tearfully told him, "Good-bye, David. I love you."

Years later, Stanley said. "I believe that Elvis simply knew the end was approaching and there was nothing he could do to change that."

Parting Words

The final words attributed to Elvis before he died are: "Okay, I won't."

He uttered them to his girlfriend Ginger Alden, while he was climbing out of bed to head for the Graceland bathroom. His words were in response to Ginger's warning not to fall asleep on the toilet. She dozed off in bed and didn't notice his absence until two hours after his death.

Bitter Pill to Swallow

Elvis was taking so many pills that his closest friends made bets on where and when the singer would die from an overdose. The members of his Memphis Mafia were prepared to smuggle the corpse of the King back to Memphis if he died somewhere else. They figured it would be easier to cover up any sordid circumstances of his death in Tennessee where Elvis truly was King.

Presley's personal physician, Dr. George Nichopoulos, prescribed huge amounts of pills to Elvis. Over the last seven months of his life, the King got prescriptions for an astounding 5,684 narcotic and amphetamine pills—an average of twenty-five per day! The day before he died, Elvis filled his last prescription—Dilaudid, Quaalude, Percodan, Dexedrine, Amytal, and Biphetamine.

Elvis may have died because he made a fatal mistake with his prescription drugs, according to Charles C. Thompson III and James P. Cole, the first reporters to see Presley's complete autopsy records.

Presley called Dr. Nichopoulos at 4 A.M. on the day of his death and asked for Dilaudid. Elvis's stepbrother Ricky Stanley picked it up and delivered it to him. However, Elvis never took the Dilaudid, according to the physician. All the tablets were accounted for in the bathroom. Toxicology tests found no trace of the drug.

However, the tests did find the equivalent of ten therapeutic doses of codeine. Elvis was allergic to codeine and would break out in a rash, become short of breath, and suffer a panic attack.

Dilaudid is made in tablet form and comes in four strengths. Tablets are round, pale yellow and labeled with numbers one through four, depending on the dosage. Empirin with codeine comes in tablets that are round, white, and labeled with numbers one through four.

It's very possible that he mistook the codeine for Dilaudid and suffered a fatal allergic reaction, say Thompson and Cole, authors of *The Death of Elvis*.

* * *

In January 1980, the Tennessee Board of Medical Examiners suspended Dr. Nichopoulos's license for three months for overprescribing addictive drugs to ten patients, including Elvis and Jerry Lee Lewis.

However, pharmacist Jack Kirsch received a much harsher punishment. The Prescription House in Memphis where Kirsch worked filled the orders from Dr. Nick. In April 1980, Kirsch swallowed a bitter pill of his own when he was ordered to give up his pharmacist's license for life.

Elvis's Funeral

Elvis was laid out in a nine hundred–pound copper-lined coffin underneath a crystal chandelier in Graceland. He was dressed in a pure white suit, light blue shirt, and white tie.

* * *

As the coffin was carried out the front door, a huge limb fell off a nearby tree and crashed to the ground. Mourners stopped in their tracks and gasped. Was this some kind of sign from the beyond, they wondered. Finally, Elvis's bodyguard Lamar Fike broke the silence by saying, "We knew you'd be back, Elvis, but not this soon."

* * *

It was a funeral fit for the King. Eleven white Cadillacs led the forty-nine-car procession to Elvis's resting place in Forest Hill Cemetery.

* * *

A whopping 3,166 floral arrangements were delivered to Graceland in tribute to the entertainer.

The funeral cost about $23,000.

The Plot against the Presley Plot

In one of the most bizarre occurrences after Presley's death, three men were arrested on suspicion of trying to tamper with his grave.

Two weeks after his death, the trio was nabbed for trespassing at Forest Hill Cemetery. Each intruder wore a dark jumpsuit and bulletproof vest and carried weapons, including hand grenades. Police felt the men were going to steal Elvis's body from the casket and hold it for a million-dollar ransom.

The men claimed they were fans who didn't believe Elvis was really dead and they wanted to open up the casket to prove to the world he was still alive. Surprisingly, the charges against the three were dropped.

May He Rest in Peace

Meditation Gardens is the beautiful grave site at Graceland where Elvis, Gladys, Vernon, and the singer's grandmother, Minnie Mae Presley, are buried.

Elvis originally joined his mother Gladys when he was laid to rest in the Presley mausoleum at Forest Hill Cemetery. But the bungled attempt to raid his casket made it clear the King could never rest in peace in such a public place. The Presley family asked for, and received, permission to move both Elvis and Gladys to the secure confines of their beloved Graceland.

* * *

Some fans believe Presley's tombstone has an error, but it doesn't.

His birth certificate reads Elvis Aron Presley, yet his gravestone at Graceland is engraved Elvis Aaron Presley. Apparently, Vernon Presley misspelled his son's middle name while listing it on the birth certificate.

The correct spelling of Elvis's middle name should have been Aaron after his daddy's pal Aaron Kennedy. Elvis later had Aron legally changed to Aaron, and that's how it appears on his tombstone.

* * *

A plaque was erected at Meditation Gardens to honor Elvis's stillborn twin, Jesse. Unfortunately, it contains the spelling error "Jessie."

Elvis's "Comeback"

Since his death on August 16, 1977, the ghost of Elvis has returned to the Graceland mansion in Memphis, according to members of his family.

Owing to his strong belief in paranormal events, it's not that much of a surprise to friends and family that Presley's ghostly presence has been seen or felt numerous times at Graceland. His ex-wife Priscilla, daughter Lisa Marie, and stepmother, Dee, have all revealed close encounters with the spirit of Elvis. The King's appearances are said to increase whenever his daughter stays at the Memphis mansion.

"Elvis was a confirmed believer in the ability of the dead to communicate with the living," Dee told reporters. "I remember Elvis telling me that he was going to be Lisa Marie's guardian angel—not only in life, but after his death."

While she was still in school, Lisa Marie confided in friends that her late father often called on her at his Graceland home. The smiling spirit would stand over Lisa Marie's bed and tell her that he would always be there for her.

Priscilla told friends that she once had a memorable midnight visit from the ghost of her ex. She was awakened from her slumber by a commotion coming from outside near the horse stables at Graceland. She gazed from her bedroom window and laid eyes on a shimmering white glow that she instinctively knew to be the spirit of Elvis. The special guest received quite a reception from his favorite mount, Rising Sun. The horse whinnied happily as if it recognized its missing master standing nearby.

Other family members claim to have seen Elvis praying near the statue of Jesus that stands in the Meditation Gardens area of Graceland. The whitish form strolls back and forth among the graves of his father, mother, and grandmother—as well as his own.

Inside the mansion, lights and other appliances will mysteriously flick on and off at all hours of the day. Then there are the eerie footsteps that are heard coming from areas of Graceland that were once favorite hangouts of the famous homeowner.

Accounts of the King's ghost at Graceland are almost endless. One Christmas holiday, several people heard the familiar tinkling of Elvis's gold-leaf grand piano. A security guard went to confront the trespassing musician, but found no one in the music room.

Another time, three sets in the television room mysteriously went on at the same moment—even though no one was in the room. On another occasion, the unmistakable sound of pool balls clacking together was heard coming from the billiards room. A check of the room failed to turn up anyone. The guard noticed that the pool balls were racked nice and neat, and Elvis's favorite cue stick had been removed from its storage space and was leaning against the table.

Family and friends aren't the only ones who've encountered the famous specter around the grounds of the fourteen-acre estate. Many tourists at Graceland claim to have met Presley's spirit—and that he's told them he's happy and well on the other side.

"There is no doubt that Elvis has come back from the dead like he promised," declared Paul Lichter, a friend of Presley's who has written two books about the star. "He told me many times he would come back from beyond the grave."

Elvis, The Friendly Ghost

People from all walks of life claim they have been helped by Presley's ghost.

Famed psychic investigator Dr. Raymond Moody Jr. traveled around the country gathering accounts of people who swear they were touched by the Elvis spirit.

"People are having visions of Elvis, just like they have visions of Jesus," Dr. Moody declared.

"One couple's dying daughter saw Elvis as she passed away," he claimed. "The girl's mother told me that as her little girl was in her last moments, her face suddenly lit up. She was holding her arms out like she was trying to reach toward someone. She said, 'Here comes Elvis.' Then she collapsed and died.

"In another incident, an unwed mother reported Elvis was standing by as her baby boy was delivered. 'Elvis came through for me when I was feeling so low,' she told me."

According to Dr. Moody, a Georgia police officer credits Presley's spirit with helping him track down his runaway teenage son.

In March 1982, the officer's troubled boy vanished. The frazzled father had a hunch his son was heading out west. Days later, Elvis's ghost appeared to the cop in a dream.

Elvis told him he too was worried about the missing boy and went on to describe in detail the rundown Los Angeles neighborhood where the youth was hiding out. Suddenly, in the dream, the cop found himself on the very L.A. street his spiritual tour guide had been talking about. Elvis and the policeman walked to a dark and dingy boarding house. Before they entered, Elvis stopped to warn the officer: "Man, your son is on drugs. You gotta get him some help."

The lawman then awoke from his eerie dream with a positive attitude about finding his son. With renewed hope, he went to California. A few days later, the father was cruising a nasty-looking neighborhood when he turned down the street that he had seen in his dream. He then slammed on his brakes because he saw the boarding house.

Now trembling with nervous excitement, the cop walked up to the door and knocked. A woman answered and, when questioned by the policeman, said his son was upstairs. The cop climbed the stairs and opened the door to his strung-out son. The wide-eyed youth gazed up from his messy bed and said he was ready to return home to Georgia— and a new life.

Later, the recovering druggie admitted to his father that he had experienced two vivid dreams about Elvis. Both times the singer's spirit assured the frightened youth that his father was on his way to rescue him.

Elvis's stepbrother Billy Stanley claims that the King returned from the dead to help him kick a bad drug habit. Stanley had gone from carrying the entertainer's personal pill kit to popping the very same drugs as the superstar. Yet, he swore Elvis pulled him back from the brink of suicide when the singer's ghost appeared to him during a drug-induced slumber in 1981.

"I know now that I'd be dead too, like Elvis, if he hadn't come down from heaven," Stanley told reporters.

Stanley said he was hooked on drugs at the age of nineteen after sneaking handfuls of pills from his stepbrother's "medicine kit"—a jewelry case where Elvis kept his amphetamines, tranquilizers, sleeping pills, and Quaaludes. In no time, the teen discovered he relied on pills to wake up and others to get to sleep. Stanley eventually added highly addictive morphine to his daily diet of drugs.

"I was doing drugs every day," he said. "And when Elvis died, I went on a mammoth, two-month binge. I set out to completely wreck myself. I just couldn't believe Elvis was dead."

After a failed suicide attempt four years after Presley's death, Stanley was loaded by friends onto a plane and flown to his brother David's home in Arlington, Texas. The vision that changed Billy's life took place ten days later.

Stanley awoke at 3:30 A.M. and found himself staring at a strange light that appeared in the far corner of his bedroom. "Framed by the light was the figure of a man, and I realized it was Elvis's ghost," Stanley recalled. "He was wearing a dazzling white jumpsuit with a gold belt. Elvis told me: 'Billy, you're destroying yourself the same way I did. I had to come back from heaven because you need me. I made a terrible mistake. Don't you make it too. I want you to stop going down the same road I traveled to oblivion. Don't make your life ugly like mine was when it ended.'

"I told Elvis, 'Okay, boss, you've got my word—no more drugs or booze.' "

Stanley felt a renewed determination to kick his hellish habit cold turkey. He flushed down the toilet all the drugs he could find and set out to break their hold on him.

Elvis, The Guardian Angel

Since his death, Elvis has been credited with healing gravely ill individuals through his music.

One such medical miracle involved a teen afflicted with an inoperable brain tumor. She thanks the King for bringing her back from the brink of death—not once, but twice!

Michele Pritzl, of Warrensville, Illinois, came out of two deep comas in the mid-1980s thanks, she says, to the continual playing of some of Presley's gospel tunes. "I am alive today by the grace of God—and with Elvis Presley's help," Michele told reporters. "Elvis is an angel from God. He is a saint to me."

The first coma struck in 1986, a year after doctors discovered that the girl's agonizing headaches were caused by a massive brain tumor. Her mother, Delores Pritzl, turned to the music of Elvis when medical treatment failed to help the teen awaken.

"She wasn't responding to anything," recalled Delores. "She was such a big Elvis fan that I bought her a headset and let her listen to Elvis's religious music. In a matter of days, she came out of the coma. It was a miracle!"

But it wouldn't be the only time. In 1988, Michele slipped into another coma when she was struck by a truck. It proved to be another King-size job for the power of Presley.

"Elvis's guiding hand came through once more," said Delores. "I played his records and twenty-eight days later she awoke. Doctors were amazed."

The Strange Signs of Presley's Death

On the day Elvis died, fans reported several bizarre happenings, according to Dr. Raymond Moody Jr.

One involved a Tennessee farmer who claimed he had been helped by Presley a few years before the King's death. The farmer said he had been in dire financial straits when Elvis heard about his problems and gave him some money and the keys to a new pickup truck.

The next time he saw Presley, the farmer was standing on a hill on his property when the singer walked toward him. The farmer couldn't figure how Elvis had driven to the farm without the singer's car being seen or heard.

The smiling star stood next to his farmer friend and noted, "I've come to say good-bye."

At that very moment, the farmer's wife yelled to her husband that the radio had just reported the death of the King. The stunned farmer turned to quiz his visitor, but Elvis had vanished into thin air.

* * *

On that same fateful day, according to Dr. Moody, a superfan decided to play a few of the many Elvis records she owned. But when she opened her big wooden stereo cabinet, she found half the vinyl discs had melted or warped into a worthless mess, while the other records were still warm to the touch. There never was a logical explanation for the mysterious meltdown.

* * *

A similar incident happened to a midwestern couple, avid Elvis fans who collected and displayed Presley merchandise, said Dr. Moody.

On the day of the King's death, they had returned to their home and discovered a statue of Elvis had fallen from its shelf and smashed on the floor. A pair of beautifully framed pictures of the star also were lying on the floor in a pile of broken glass. There was no sign of a break-in. Minutes later, they turned on the television and heard the startling news that Elvis was dead.

The upset couple had a difficult time collecting their wits as they pieced the statue back together. But their ordeal was far from over. That night they were in bed when a loud thump came from the "Elvis Room" downstairs. They found the statue was once again a pile of fragments on the floor. This time, an entire shelf of souvenirs had broken free from the wall and dumped its precious contents into a sad heap.

"I don't believe that death is the end.
Reincarnation has got to be real."

Notable Notes

When Elvis was four years old, his father, Vernon, served nine months of a three-year sentence on a penal farm after he pleaded guilty to forging the check of a local farmer. Vernon had sold the farmer a hog for four dollars, but then altered the check to read forty dollars.

Elvis's mother, Gladys, picked cotton and took in other people's laundry to support herself and her young son during Vernon's incarceration.

* * *

Vernon Presley once told young Elvis: "I never knew a guitar player that was worth a damn!"

The words struck a chord with Elvis, who never let his father forget them. The scathing statement was inscribed on a plaque that hung on the wall at Graceland. It was Elvis's way of saying, "Next time, Daddy, don't be cruel."

* * *

Traveling on commercial airlines proved to be a royal pain for the King. Yet until Elvis could afford his own jet, he was forced to share rides with his adoring public. In order to ease the pressure of such trips, Elvis staffers would use an alias while booking his flights. Many ticket agents booked Dr. John Carpenter without knowing the seat would be filled by the singing star himself.

* * *

Tom Parker wasn't the only colonel in Elvis's life. Tennessee governor Buford Ellington conferred the honorary title of colonel on Elvis himself in 1961.

* * *

Elvis stuttered! The speech impediment surfaced when Elvis spoke fast or was nervous. The stuttering was documented for posterity in Elvis flicks *Kissin' Cousins* and *Wild in the Country*.

* * *

Elvis may have been Big Man in America, but college officials at UCLA nixed his plans to be Big Man on Campus.

The King wanted to enroll for some night classes at the university after discovering the joys of reading and learning. But school officials thought his presence would be much too disruptive for the other students.

* * *

Graceland has become a giant tourist attraction since Presley's death there. The mansion ranks second to the White House in the number of annual visitors to a private home. About a half-million people shuffle through Graceland each year.

* * *

Seventeen portraits of Elvis were hanging throughout Graceland at the time of his death. (It's not known how many were velvet.)

* * *

Elvis owned twenty pairs of pajamas. When he died, he was wearing a blue top and yellow bottoms.

* * *

"Butch" was the slang word for milk that Elvis used from childhood until his death.

* * *

Elvis's favorite film was *Dr. Strangelove: Or How I Learned to Stop Worrying and Love the Bomb.* It featured one of the King's favorite actors, Peter Sellers, in three different roles. Elvis watched the 1964 British-made film at least fifty times in his life.

* * *

The name Elvis is derived from the Norse word "alviss," which means all wise.

* * *

Think your taxes are bad? Elvis once paid 91 percent of his annual income to the Internal Revenue Service. The King didn't want to be bothered with figuring out his own taxes so he allowed the IRS that honor. Without any significant tax shelters, Elvis was socked every year.

* * *

In 1974, Elvis played a grueling 152 dates and grossed in excess of seven million dollars. Yet at the end of the year, the free-spending singer was forced to dip into his own reserves for another $700,000 to make ends meet.

* * *

Elvis banked at the National Bank of Commerce in Memphis. The singer signed his checks E.A. Presley. At the time of his death, Elvis had $1,055,173.69 in his no-interest checking account.

* * *

Las Vegas optician Dennis Roberts created more than four hundred pairs of prescription sunglasses for the nearsighted Elvis. His sunglass collection was valued at $60,000.

* * *

Elvis was touched by people who were suffering. Once, after a nurse informed him of a little girl named Karen who was a victim of cerebral palsy, Elvis began writing to her. The two became pen pals until she died at the age of ten.

* * *

Elvis sometimes used his cash to test the honesty of guests at Graceland. He once spread thousand-dollar bills across a bed, then arranged for each person to spend some time alone in the room with the tempting stash of cash. None of the guests took any money.

* * *

One of Presley's first cars was a red and black German Messerschmidt model he bought in 1956. The King never kept his personal cars for long. He soon traded his Messerschmidt to Memphis clothing store owner Bernard Lansky.

In exchange, Elvis got to select a new wardrobe from the racks of wild-colored out-fits offered by Lansky. It took Elvis over two and a half hours to come up with just the right clothes to complete the bizarre trade.

* * *

Elvis loved words. He once handed the members of his entourage dictionaries. At night, each member of the Memphis Mafia would choose a word for the entire crew to dis-cuss, pronounce, and learn its proper usage.

* * *

Elvis suffered through a string of nicknames he hated. As a boy, he was called "Elvy," which he despised. But it still was a lot less stinging than his other moniker—"Mama's Boy."

Later, when his singing career took off, Presley endured several silly labels such as: "The Hillbilly Frank Sinatra" and "Elvis Pretzel," the latter attributed to Humphrey Bogart.

Even Colonel Parker got into the act when he proclaimed his skyrocketing star "The Nation's First Atomic-Powered Singer." Elvis rarely commented on these nicknames.

But he really took exception to "Elvis the Pelvis." The singer complained: "That's about the most stupid thing I've heard from so-called intelligent adults."

Among the nicknames that didn't bother Elvis were: E, Big E, Big El, The Bopping Hillbilly, The Cat, The Chief, Mr. Dynamite, and The King.

* * *

When Dewey Phillips—the first disc jockey to play and plug Elvis's debut record—died, Presley didn't forget him. The King went to Phillips' s funeral in Millington, Tennessee, where the D.J. had worked for a small radio station. At the services, Elvis got an unexplainable case of the giggles and couldn't stop, much to his own embarrassment.

* * *

Early in his career, Elvis had such a bad sleepwalking habit that for a while he wasn't allowed to sleep alone. Gene Smith, an aide to the star, had the task of bunking with Presley at Graceland to prevent any possible injury while sleepwalking.

* * *

According to Presley's personal physician, members of the singer's entourage had to endure the "sweat smell" of Presley's success.

Dr. George Nichopoulos said the King had a royal dislike for soap and water. He preferred instead to simply sponge off. This practice led to problems with nasty bacterial infections for the man famous for his sweaty stage performances. In fact, he sweat so much that vendors would hock vials of his perspiration wrung out of towels that Elvis used!

Of course, no one dared raise a stink over Presley's poor hygiene habits, since the sweat of his talented brow was what paid their bills.

* * *

When you think of Elvis, you immediately picture him with his sexy jet-black pompadour. The truth is Presley had to hit the bottle to get that unforgettable look because he was born with blondish-brown hair. The entertainer began dying his hair black as a hairy homage to fellow singing star Roy Orbison.

In the last few years of his life, Presley's brown hair was turning gray. So Memphis Mafia member Charlie Hodge undertook the colorful task of keeping Elvis's hair black. Every few weeks the men would retire to the bathroom for a dye job.

"Ain't nowhere else in the world where you can go from driving a truck to driving a Cadillac overnight. Nowhere."